Reflections on Life and Liberty

Michael Quinn Sullivan

Reflections on Life and Liberty

© 2023 Michael Quinn Sullivan.

All rights reserved. No part of this publication may be reproduced, distributed, or transmitted in any form or by any means, including photocopying, recording, or other electronic or mechanical methods, without the prior written permission of the publisher, except as permitted by U.S. copyright law.

CNG Publishing
P.O. Box 248, Leander, Texas 78646

ISBN: 979-8-9878490-0-2 (eBook)
ISBN: 979-8-9878490-1-9 (Paperback)
ISBN: 979-8-9878490-2-6 (Hardcover)

Contents

Introduction vii
PART I 1
Why We Fight 3
What We Tolerate 5
Blind Men 8
Cleaning Up 10
Be Strong; Fear Not 12
Fighting Honorably 14
Fighting Faithfully 16
Fighting Is What Counts 18
Outnumbered, Outgunned 20
Defined… Or Defining? 23
Truth to Power 25
PART II 29
Be a Hammer 31
Be a Troubler 35
A Joyful Responsibility 37
Giving Thanks 39
Cheerful Warriors 42
Keep Going 45
Let Them Whine 47
Liberty Is Fragile 49
Sticks and Stones 51

Watch Your Language!	53
They Are Not Mainstream	56
Stop Laying Around	59
The Cost of Betraying Our Heritage	61
Being Trustworthy	63
You Don't Need a Plan	65
The Army You Need	67
Praying for the Wrong People	69
Access for What?	72
PART III	75
Stop Making Their Excuses	77
Who Are the Idiots?	79
When Someone Tells You Who They Are…	81
Stop Being Nice	84
Who Do You Serve?	86
Make Them Fear You	88
Action Beats Rhetoric	90
Confusing Volume and Mass	92
What We Trust In	95
Political Corruption Is Our Fault	98
Don't Get Distracted	101
Just a Small Bit of Liberty?	103
Kings Die	105
People-Pleasers	107

Hypocrites' Chair	109
Rule of Law	111
The Wrong Response	113
Two-Card Monte	115
You Just Don't Understand	118
What Do You Expect?	120
At the Crossroads	122
Acknowledgements	125
About the Author	127

INTRODUCTION

This compilation is for people who have been, are, or will be, in the fight for liberty in our Republic. It is for those who want to make a difference and throw their "lives, fortunes, and sacred honor" into the mix. It is for those who know the fight is important.

Most of all, it is for those who have started to feel a little burned out.

These short reflections started not with the goal of sharing them with others, but because I was feeling weighed down from being in the fight.

Not weighed down in the sense of being tired, but I had become so accustomed to fighting that I was beginning to forget why I was fighting, and for what. I learned this is all too common. It can be wearying, and dangerous.

History provides guideposts. As the author of Ecclesiastes reminds us, "There is nothing new under the sun."

For 400 years, Israel lived as a self-governing people —sometimes with peace and prosperity, and other times with calamity and frustration. Time and time again, we see that their "success" and "failure" as a self-governing people was related to how zealous they were in faithfully serving Him and His people. Along the way, they became comfortable. Too comfortable, perhaps. They had lost their zeal, and their fight.

Just as it can be wearying to always be in the fight, oppression results when we stop being willing to fight. If character is what you do when no one is watching, tyranny is what we get when no one is participating.

That's what happened in Israel. The people decided they wanted to look like everyone else, and not be inconvenienced by having to govern themselves. They asked for a king. They were told by God through the prophet Samuel how kings would tax them, take their land and children, and engage in meaningless wars. The people rejected God, and got their king.

And things went downhill fast. For the next thousand years, Israel was a ruled-over land and people. In the 2nd century B.C. during the time of the Maccabees, they had—and squandered—their last opportunity for meaningful self-governance.

In that period arose the Zealots. These were people zealous for self-governance, for independence from the rule of Ptolemy, the Seleucids, and especially the Romans. Some of the Zealots became early followers of Jesus of Nazareth, who gave them something different about which to be zealous.

Many, though, were zealous to be... zealous. They were in the fight because they were in the fight, and they fought because they were fighters. They wanted to throw off Roman rule, yet being so consumed by that fight, they could no longer articulate what they wanted instead.

As mentioned above, I saw that in myself. So—appropriately—on a trip to Israel I began writing early versions of some of these reflections as a way to ask myself why I was doing any of it. In Scripture, in the stories of our forefathers, I rediscovered my love for the fight. More importantly, I rediscovered what I have been fighting for.

A little later, we started publishing more refined versions every couple of weeks at our news website, *Texas Scorecard*.

Now they are published weekly, often with an accompanying podcast on a similar theme.

Being in the fight can be wearying. To avoid being like the foolish zealots, we must force ourselves to take a break and remind ourselves why we fight.

Which is where this collection begins...

PART I
BEING SELF-GOVERNING

"It is easier to find people fit to govern themselves than people to govern others. Every man is the best, the most responsible, judge of his own advantage."

– British statesman and philosopher, Lord Acton

WHY WE FIGHT
Does the right to govern ourselves matter?

We have forgotten just how extraordinary it is to be Americans. We have allowed the notion of being an American to become common. But the fact is, America is anything but common—especially in its origins.

British Prime Minister Margaret Thatcher understood that. She once said, "Europe was created by history. America was created by philosophy."

But it was not an esoteric philosophy of learned men in ivory towers. No, it was the practical philosophy of a practical people driven by their faith and experience.

In the early 1840s, a young historian named Mellen Chamberlain sought out one of the last surviving participants in the Battle of Concord to ask him about that experience. The minuteman's name was Levi Preston, who was 91 at the time of their conversation.

(Mr. Chamberlain later recorded the interview in his work, *John Adams, the Statesman of the American Revolution.*)

Chamberlain asked Preston why he had fought the British. The answers weren't what the historian expected, for Preston did not speak about oppressive British rule, the stamp tax, the tea tax, or the writings of the philosophers like John Locke.

"Well, then," asked Chamberlain, the exasperation leaping from the page, "why did you fight?"

Preston's answer still takes my breath away: "Young man, what we meant in going for those redcoats was this: We always had governed ourselves, and we always meant to and they meant that we shouldn't."

It was this concept of self-government, so natural to Levi Preston and his contemporaries, that changed the world. It is at the practical root of American exceptionalism. It's why our nation has thrived, even as older and more established nations withered and passed into the dustbin of history.

America is exceptional because we, the people, govern ourselves. Levi Preston and his generation had the moral courage to do what they knew to be right: reject an offer of tyranny so that self-governance could thrive.

We do not elect almighty leaders, but public servants. We cannot tolerate unlimited government or make allowance for the divine right of politicians.

We govern ourselves, thank you very much.

Yet self-governance is fragile; it only exists to the extent we continue to participate in it. If self-government is to continue, if liberty is to flourish, if we are to remain independent, we must be informed, engaged, and active citizens.

We must, every day, intentionally fight for the right to govern ourselves.

WHAT WE TOLERATE
Self-governance starts with governing ourselves.

As a personal and civic virtue, tolerance can be a tricky attitude to master without becoming morally rudderless.

But as a governing practice and a civic virtue, the modern implementation of tolerance is a deadly vice. Even typing these words makes me feel disloyal to 50 years of enculturation in the public adoration of "tolerance."

We are allowed in the polite company of the ruling elite only when we agree to "tolerate" that which should otherwise be intolerable. To enjoy the peace of the elite, we must stop pursuing public righteousness.

Sure, it is alright in the privacy of your home to do moral things and think moral thoughts ... but we are told you must not allow that morality to influence your public life and decisions.

The purveyors of sin and vice demand we "tolerate" their activities. They know that, with time and exposure, the solid mooring of morality can be worn away. Public tolerance becomes acquiescence, which slips neatly into participation.

Think back to God's command to His people after He freed them from bondage. He told them to conquer the Promised Land, to completely destroy the temples and altars to the false gods, and to drive out all worshippers of those false gods. To be a self-governing people under His law, God told them, they needed to drive out those things incompatible with His righteousness.

Time and again, the people would always start to obey; they wanted the benefits. But then they would capitulate. They would decide it was easier to tolerate the evil in their midst than obey God. Time and again, their tolerance of false gods and false worship led to their enslavement and misery ... often by the adherents of the false religions they were tolerating.

"The people of Israel did what was evil in the sight of the Lord." We find that phrase repeated time and again. And what they "did" started with tolerating the presence of evil.

Capitulation to sin begins with a toleration of sinful activity.

We've all heard variations of the truism found in 1 Corinthians 15:33: "Do not be deceived: 'Bad company ruins good morals.'" The very next sentence, which is just as true, continues: "Wake up from your drunken stupor, as is right, and do not go on sinning."

Any critique of society's tolerance of "bad company" is usually countered by a variation of "Jesus was so tolerant. Why can't you be more like Jesus?" It sounds so spiritual.

Do they mean the Jesus who overturned tables outside the temple and ran out the money-changers with a whip? The Jesus who called the political leaders of the day a "brood of vipers"?

That Jesus, the Jesus of the Bible, isn't welcome in the 2020s. Nowhere in Scripture do you find a Jesus who coddles unrepentant sinners. Nowhere do you find a Jesus who tolerates sin. You repeatedly find a Jesus who meets sinners where they are and then tells them to "sin no more." Some do and follow Him; others leave.

"Sin no more" is loving the sinner so much as to not tolerate the sin. By tolerating sin, we are condemning people to lives of pain and misery—and perhaps worse.

Self-governance starts with governing ourselves and helping those around us to do likewise. If we expect to enjoy the benefits of living in a righteous land, we must set aside political tolerance and pursue lives of righteousness.

BLIND MEN

Being blind is bad enough, but blindly following rules established by the elite is worse.

The Gospel of Jesus was, and remains, highly subversive. We lose sight of just how subversive with the comfort of 2,000 years of hindsight, and even the creep of a new status quo. Yet the forces of cronyism, legalism, and establishmentarianism are just as prevalent today—and so is the radical need for Jesus.

I'm constantly reminded of that when I walk around Israel and read through the pages of Scripture.

Take, for example, the Pool of Siloam, which was discovered early in the 21st century during archeological excavations. This is where Jesus brought sight to a man blind since birth. The Gospel of John, chapter 9, records the story.

Jesus "anointed the man's eyes with the mud and said to him, 'Go, wash in the pool of Siloam'... So he went and washed and came back seeing."

The man, as one might expect, was overjoyed. His life was literally changed in an instant, evident for all to see.

Yet the establishment enforcers, the Pharisees—who were universally praised by the Jews of the day as political and religious heroes—were aghast. Their complaint was that the healing had taken place on the Sabbath. But you get the impression in John's account they were more upset because Jesus had done it without their permission. Jesus refused to conform to their rules; He was too busy following God's law.

Meanwhile, the formerly blind man was indignant. He could see! Yet the Pharisees were more concerned with enforcing their peculiar interpretation of the Ten Commandments than in rejoicing in an obvious miracle. And because the man would not reject the gift of sight or the One who had given it, they labeled—and libeled—him as one "born in utter sin."

Things have not changed. Those who would do good —such as innovators disrupting an industry with lower prices and better services, or volunteers feeding the hungry without bureaucratic approval—find themselves under assault from the minions of an administrative state operating on behalf of entrenched incumbent actors.

And those who try to tell the truth about the benefits they received from the disruptors? They are attacked with even greater ferocity. They are denigrated as unfaithful, as cheaters, or worse.

With whom would we side? The blind man couldn't unsee the world after being given sight; he knew what was true. Should he have backed down? And what will we do? Will we be even more pitiable men, self-blinded to truth?

We can chose not to ruffle feathers, perpetuate the status quo, and leave people in darkness... Or we can join in a glorious disruption that brings light to the world.

CLEANING UP
Corruption in government won't fix itself.

We all heard it from our mothers: "Cleanliness is next to godliness." Though come to think of it, I'm not sure that ever properly motivated me to actually clean my room as a kid. (Sorry, mom!)

Thanks to sin, none of us—like petulant children before bedtime—really want to be clean on our own. But thanks to God, we can be.

The notion of cleanliness pervades Scripture, specifically the realization that none of us are clean enough by God's standards. That's why a tree-lined bend along the Jordan River is so meaningful. It's recognized as the place where John baptized his cousin, Jesus.

Jesus' baptism marked the beginning of His public ministry. On the one hand, it seems strange that Jesus—literally, the Son of God, the Incarnate Word, the Messiah—"needed" to be baptized. But the fact He was points all the more clearly to our own need to do so. Even if we follow it imperfectly, we should try to follow His example.

Let's be clear: Baptism isn't about physical cleanliness, but rather the state of our heart. Just as a dirty room cannot clean itself (another mom-based truism), neither can our dirty hearts. Making our spiritual lives "clean" takes an act of God, as expressed outwardly through baptism.

John Adams once wrote, "Our Constitution was made only for a moral and religious People. It is wholly inadequate to the government of any other." So if we want to clean up government, let us pray for a cleansing revival of the people.

In our self-governing Republic, we cannot bemoan corruption in government and hope someone else will do something about it. It's up to us, and sometimes we have to start doing the work alone where we are.

A dirty room won't clean itself, and neither will a dirty government.

BE STRONG; FEAR NOT

There may be fearsome fights ahead, but it doesn't mean we should be fearful.

It seems everyone wants to be a victim. Everyone wears weakness as a badge of secular honor, and demands others validate their fears. May I suggest a different way?

Scattered throughout the Old and New testaments of the Bible are variations of the phrases "be strong," "be courageous," 'take courage," and "fear not." It is almost like God knows the whole "I'm a victim" thing is spiritual poison.

It also explains why the purveyors of cultural rot prefer you to adopt the fatalistic posture of a victim. People who cower and cringe rarely fight back. The political elite want us to live lives full of anxiety, so that we can be more easily controlled.

The words of Isaiah still speak to us: "Say to those who have an anxious heart, 'Be strong; fear not! Behold, your God will come with vengeance, with the recompense of God. He will come and save you.'"

Rather than live shadowy lives as cowering supplicants, we are called to walk in confidence.

As Paul wrote in his letter to the Romans, "If God is for us, who can be against us?" He later adds, "For I am sure that neither death nor life, nor angels nor rulers, nor things present nor things to come, nor powers, nor height nor depth, nor anything else in all creation, will be able to separate us from the love of God in Christ Jesus our Lord."

Yes, there are some fearsome fights ahead of us, but it doesn't mean we should be fearful of them. When the people of God were preparing to cross into the Promised Land, God charged their leader Joshua: "Be strong and courageous... I will be with you."

Throughout their conquest of the land, you find Joshua and the people echoing that phrase back and forth as words of encouragement.

So should we.

Be strong and courageous; fear not.

The years ahead present a great many opportunities to fight and struggle for the cause of self-governance in our Republic. Take courage from the knowledge that you are not alone in this struggle, that other men and women are likewise doing what they can, where they can, to advance liberty.

What is asked of us is not victory, but only to be strong and courageous.

FIGHTING HONORABLY
Even when it is inconvenient, even in the darkness, even when our friends tell us otherwise.

As the saying goes, "Context is king." Nowhere have I seen that so practically displayed as in Israel, where passages from the Bible spring to life in the context of their physical locations. Nagging questions are answered with a glance and a footstep.

Few biblical vignettes puzzled me more over the years than that found in 1 Samuel 24. Let me try to set the stage. King Saul and his men were chasing David—knowing the young man was ordained by God to be Israel's ruler. David and his men fled into the wilderness region known as Ein Gedi, and were hiding in a cave. As it happened, it was into that very cave which King Saul entered to "relieve himself."

David and his men conspired about whether to attack the king. How easy it would have been! After all, Saul was trying to kill them!

As it happened, David snipped a piece of Saul's robe (without the king's knowledge), but regretted it as a cowardly act and forbade his men from taking action.

So it always puzzled me... How were David and his men not seen? How were they not heard? How could David have moved close enough to cut Saul's robe without the king knowing it?

Well, very easily, it turns out. The cave features a massive waterfall and raging stream that carved the cave from fragile rock. Back then, the cave would have been pitch black, the floor littered with man-sized chunks of rock. Several dozen men could have been standing there yelling, and they never would have been seen or heard. And, to put it delicately, one would have to carefully disrobe before going about the king's task that day.

When you stand there, the story makes perfect sense. All sorts of nefarious actions could have happened in that space.

While Saul was a dishonorable king, David did not want to begin his own kingship in a dishonorable way. While Saul would probably have thought nothing of killing David with his pants down (or robe up), David wanted Saul to keep his dignity. David wanted to honor God, even in the darkness of a cave against a man who wanted him dead.

When my wife and I stood at the mouth of the cave, looking down at the Jordan River below and marveling at the beauty of the place, it was hard not to think of the pressure to "win at all costs."

The lesson at Ein Gedi reminds us that the ends cannot be justification for the means. If we want to be honorable men, we must behave honorably—even when it is inconvenient, even in the darkness, even when our friends tell us otherwise. As a self-governing people, we must first be able to govern ourselves.

That is, perhaps, the most important context for each of us.

FIGHTING FAITHFULLY
Our job is to be faithful to the fight.

When most of us hear the name "Magdala," we might possibly connect it with the New Testament's Mary Magdalene (or Mary of Magdala, same person). But the city itself has a lot to tell us about faithfulness in the face of defeat.

During the last century B.C. and the first century A.D., Jews chaffed under Roman rule. Sure, some made off pretty well working with the Romans. Many others, though, yearned for the kind of self-governing independence that their ancestors had been promised but squandered when they demanded that God give them a king.

Like swarming gnats, a couple of minor would-be insurrections had been crushed over the years.

By the latter half of the first century A.D., however, frustration was hitting a fever pitch.

The result was the Great Revolt. The region around the Sea of Galilee was a hotbed of activity for the Zealot rebels—those Jews who wanted to overthrow the Romans. (With what, exactly, they would replace Roman rule was a somewhat fuzzy concept. The Zealots had become so accustomed to being zealously opposed to Rome that their zealotry became an end unto itself.)

Magdala was a fishing village of little note... except as a gathering place for the Jewish rebels. We know this because it was also the hometown to the Jewish leader known to us as the Roman historian Josephus Flavius. In 67 B.C., the Romans laid siege to Magdala. Some inhabitants fled after it fell, but most were murdered by the Romans. For Texans, think of a massacre like Goliad or the Alamo... but probably worse.

The archeological ruins uncovered in recent years have found city streets still barricaded against the coming Roman forces. Here's the thing, hastily stacked stones and trash were never going to stop the Romans.

It did, however, send a signal that this revolt wasn't going to be put down so easily.

The Romans learned at Magdala that the zeal of the Jewish rebels would be costly for all involved.

The Romans did finally (several years later) crush the revolt. Towns like Magdala faded from history, literally wiped from the earth by the might of the Roman war machine. We remember the Alamo and Goliad because we won; would either place be remembered if the Texas Revolution had failed? Probably not.

The people of Magdala were just as heroic as the men at the Alamo. So for us Magdala is a reminder that no matter how noble the struggle, losing is always a real possibility. We fight not knowing if we'll win, but if we feel so called we must fight nonetheless—and fight zealously.

Our reward may be victory, the cause a glorious success. Or we may fade into the dark recesses of time, a footnote in history. If our cause is just and we are following God's will, either outcome should be acceptable.

We must proceed with the dedication and bravery of the men of the Alamo and the people of Magdala. The choice is ours.

FIGHTING IS WHAT COUNTS
Independence Day celebrates the first, necessary step in winning: deciding to fight.

This might offend some, but there was no difference in the 13 colonies between July 3, 1776, and July 5, 1776. By all appearances, the American colonies were no more free, no more independent. The governing structures had not noticeably changed.

So what makes the Fourth of July so special?

Think about it. We don't celebrate October 19, 1781, the date the War for American independence ended. There are no parades commemorating September 3, 1783, when the Treaty of Paris formally concluded the war.

No, we celebrate the Fourth of July. That is the day when our Founding Fathers firmly, finally, and officially committed themselves—their lives, their fortunes, their sacred honor—to the cause of American independence. Now, make no mistake; many of them had done so personally and individually weeks, months, even years earlier.

The Fourth of July is when they did it formally. They acknowledged to each other and a "candid world" that they were dissolving their political bands with England.

We celebrate the Fourth of July because that is the day they said it together with one voice. We celebrate their commitment to the fight. We recognize that in the most important ways, by choosing to declare their independence, they had already achieved it.

Holocaust survivor Viktor Frankl reflected on his time in Auschwitz, writing: "Everything can be taken from a man but one thing: the last of the human freedoms — to choose one's attitude in any given set of circumstances, to choose one's own way."

Just as Frankl refused to submit his humanity to the Nazi captors, so our Founding Fathers chose to be free of English tyranny. That choice, the faithfulness to the fight, is what counts.

Holy Scripture tells us that, through Christ, we are already free. Through Him, we have attained the truest independence and victory over death. Yes, we still must struggle with sin and rail against the fallen world. We are called to be faithful, to press on in the knowledge of our eternal freedom.

Nearly all of our Founding Fathers were men of faith; they understood that the struggle in which they were to engage may or may not be successful in the eyes of the world. That didn't matter; they achieved freedom in their choice, declared on the Fourth of July. The fight ahead was merely the necessary consequence of being faithful.

On Independence Day, we celebrate their commitment to the ideals of self-governance. On Independence Day, we celebrate their willingness to put their convictions to the test for themselves and for us.

OUTNUMBERED, OUTGUNNED
A self-governing people can overcome the odds.

If you are encouraged by those who were outnumbered, outgunned, and out-trained, yet still won the day, the month of October offers two great examples.

The first was the Battle of Gonzales on Oct. 2, 1835. The Mexican government told the independence-minded people of Gonzales that soldiers would be taking away the town's cannon. The people had other ideas and stood resolute against the action.

They hoisted a flag declaring "Come and Take It" over the town. The people of Gonzales were determined to govern themselves, which meant maintaining their ability to protect themselves.

A short battle between the men of Gonzales and the better trained Mexican soldiers ended with the people victorious—and keeping their cannon—while the defeated Mexicans beat a hasty retreat.

Fast forward 140 years, and 7,000 miles due east, to the Golan Heights, at the border of Israel and Syria. There you find the Valley of Tears, where a severely outnumbered Israeli force bested the Syrian army during the outset of the Yom Kippur War in October 1973.

The Syrians and their Arab allies—Egypt and Jordan—planned to invade Israel ahead of Yom Kippur, a Jewish holiday. In the critical Golan Heights, fewer than 100 Israeli tanks stood against more than 500 Soviet-made tanks and 1,900 other pieces of deadly military hardware.

As the action began to unfold, the Israeli commanders on the ground didn't wait for instructions from distant superiors who were no doubt enjoying the holiday. They went to work defending their country.

After four days of intense fighting, approximately 70 of the 100 Israeli tanks were lost... but the Syrians were in retreat. The Syrian forces lost nearly all their tanks and armored vehicles in a psychologically humiliating defeat. The outcome of the two-week Yom Kippur War mirrored that decisive tank battle in the Golan Heights, with the outnumbered Israelis fighting off the Arab world.

The country's main intelligence operations hadn't forecasted the attacks, among other reasons, because of the way their bureaucracy processed reports for later analysis. Yet individual commanders on the ground saw what was happening and acted accordingly, taking advantage of the decentralized nature of the Israeli military at the time.

Self-governance as an operating model, based on Old Testament instructions from God, forms the basis of Israeli society even if it is not necessarily a part of their modern governing institutions. Without that ingrained sense of self-governance, the Battle of the Valley of Tears and the Yom Kippur War would have gone very differently for Israel.

In Texas and the rest of the United States, our Founding Fathers explicitly sought to frame our government in a way that emphasized self-governance by strictly limiting the powers of government. They understood that while a strong leader—a ruler, a king, a dictator—might allow his subjects varying degrees of freedom, only a self-governing people can truly act in the best interest of their communities.

That spirit of self-governance was on full display at Gonzales where the people were unwilling to live as unarmed serfs. They wanted to govern, and protect, themselves. And they were willing to be faithful to the fight.

The extent to which we value our liberty is the extent to which we will fight daily to protect our legacy of self-governance.

DEFINED... OR DEFINING?

Those who ignore both the jeers and the cheers of the world are happier and more productive.

Life comes at us pretty fast, and there are two kinds of people: those who are defined by their circumstances, and those who choose to define themselves in their circumstances.

With certain exceptions, we generally cannot control the circumstances of life. Sure, we can refuse that drink at a bar, we can avoid being with a certain kind of people, or choose not to engage in a particular sort of activity. But for the most part, the circumstances of life slam into us.

A foreign ruler's decision to invade another country upsets the global economy, triggering a recession that forces your employer out of business. Some cabal of politicians from other parts of the country conspire to push legislation you oppose and enact policies you believe to be detrimental to the pursuit of happiness. You get the point; many things in the world happen to us outside of our control.

What we can control is our attitude, our outlook, and our reaction to those circumstances. We can be defined by them, or we can define them by the attitude and posture we chose to take despite them.

In the early 19th century, the English poet William Wordsworth described the "Character of the Happy Warrior" in an ode to Lord Admiral Horatio Nelson. Having already lost an arm and an eye in a previous battle, Nelson nonetheless refused to give up the fight or his good humor. Nelson was eventually killed by a sniper while leading a successful battle, inspiring his men to even greater success.

The happy warrior, Wordsworth wrote, "looks forward, persevering to the last… and, while the mortal mist is gathering, draws his breath in confidence of Heaven's applause."

In my experience, those who let themselves be defined by the prevailing circumstances generally, in this fallen world, are a cheerless and grumbling lot. They look back on times that were rarely as wonderful as they remember, and proceed to spend their time mourning its passing.

On the other hand, those who ignore both the jeers and the cheers of the world are much happier. They look forward joyfully to what they can achieve in their circumstances, or the contribution they can make in the advancement of their ideas.

The difference is found in the daily choice of personal perspective. Will our attitude be dictated by others, or will we govern ourselves?

As a self-governing people, we must learn from the past and understand with clarity the present. Yet even more importantly, we must choose to be driven—happily—by our role in shaping and defining the possibilities of the future.

TRUTH TO POWER
Government bureaucracies may feed the stomach, but they crush the soul.

America is losing its founding sense of self-governance because our churches have gone silent; or, worse, become shills for the welfare state.

When the Hellenists were kicked from Israel in the second and first century B.C., the fight was led by a priest and his sons. The American Revolution was famously staffed by pastors who gave up their pulpits to serve their flocks in battle. The Civil Rights movement of the 1950s and '60s was nurtured in churches.

Yet the last 40 years have seen American pulpits go increasingly quiet on issues that matter most. On any given Sunday, pastors can be found waxing eloquent about the derivations of Greek words or amusing their congregation with self-help anecdotes like a part-time comedian during open-mic night.

Too many pastors have become unwilling to speak uncomfortable truths in the face of governing power. They do not want to risk offending the sensibilities of the soft leftists in their congregations or the hard leftists in government bureaucracies.

Yet questioning earthly powers, and upsetting the governing status quo of the religious and political elite, was all part and parcel of Jesus' ministry. That same sensibility has been effectively educated out of most mainline seminaries.

Today, churches often reflect the government dictates and secular mores rather than standing apart from them. In the name of "peace and purity" in the church, a large number of pastors avoid confrontation with a soft capitulation. Criticism of government is verboten. Sermons against confiscatory taxes, abortion, and same-sex marriage might scare away "seekers" and are thus avoided.

A friend who attended a very conservative seminary told me he was distressed by the sheer number of students who subsisted on government programs.

He was frustrated that while the church is called to care for the poor, pastors emerging from seminaries—having been enculturated into the welfare state—would too readily embrace the idea that church money should be reserved for esoteric pursuits. As he said mockingly, they had lived on government handouts and turned out just fine.

The biblical call for Christians to care personally for the least among us is at the heart of a self-governing people. Or it should be.

Offloading the messiness of practical compassion to a faceless bureaucracy might be convenient, but it fails to uphold the dignity of the individual being served. And it completely ignores the mandate for Christians to practice acts of mercy.

We have relegated "loving our neighbor" to "providing a convenient app for getting a list of government services."

British historian Tom Holland hit on this in a commentary for *The Telegraph*:

"Parroting the slogans of the Department of Health and Social Care may conceivably help save lives—but it seems unlikely to win many souls.... If [churches] are not to seem merely eccentric branch offices of the welfare state, they need to recapture their confidence, and take a risk: the risk of seeming odd."

Jesus had no trouble being odd. He called odd men to be His disciples. Following God is, indeed, very odd to those who hate Him. The wisdom of God is treated as foolishness by sinful men. We must reject the pursuit of cultural approval and embrace the oddness of God if we are to serve Him faithfully. And it is only by serving God that we can truly love our neighbors.

Churches—pastors and parishioners alike—must reject the welfare state and reassert their God-given role in fighting for the weak, the downtrodden, and the rejected. Government bureaucracies may feed the stomach, but they crush the soul.

America's legacy as a self-governing people will survive and thrive only to the extent our churches are willing to speak truthfully, even forcefully, to secular power.

PART II
ACTING AS CITIZENS

"Bad men cannot make good citizens. It is impossible that a nation of infidels or idolaters should be a nation of freemen. It is when a people forget God that tyrants forge their chains. A vitiated state of morals, a corrupted public conscience, is incompatible with freedom. No free government, or the blessings of liberty, can be preserved to any people but by a firm adherence to justice, moderation, temperance, frugality, and virtue; and by a frequent recurrence to fundamental principles."

– Patrick Henry

BE A HAMMER

Don't let liberty be sacrificed on the self-interested altars politicians erect to themselves.

As a Protestant, I grew up without the Maccabees. The two books of the Maccabees are among what my Catholic friends call the "deuterocanonical" portion of the Bible. For more than a thousand years, Christians have debated—and will continue to debate—the theological significance of those books.

Yet all of us would benefit from understanding the Maccabean period.

Judea was going through a period of Hellenization, trapped between the Syrians and Egyptians—both kingdoms having been influenced by Alexander the Great. By 200 B.C., the Syrian Seleucids had taken over Judea, and their culture took root among the upper-class Jews in Jerusalem. These were Jews ready to be done with the law and other religious trappings of Judaism. They wanted to be accepted—socially and economically—into the kingdom of their latest masters.

That didn't sit well with observant Jews, particularly those living in the countryside. They saw two enemies: their backstabbing countrymen, and the Hellenistic Seleucids whose king had—for a bribe—unceremoniously forced out the rightful high priest.

The country rabble didn't like it. A village priest, Mattathias the Hasmonean, and his sons organized a revolt. The youngest of them, Judah (sometimes written as

Judas), emerged as an able military leader. He was given the name "Maccabee"—drawn from the word for "hammer"—in recognition of his fierce and heroic leadership in battle. He successfully led a rag-tag volunteer force in what we would recognize as guerrilla warfare against a much stronger opponent.

Yet the revolt almost ended at Mount Arbel in central Israel. On seeing an amassed Seleucidian army before battle, thousands of his rebels simply fled. Just 800 were left behind, many of whom were killed in the fighting, including Judah himself.

Inspired by the example of their younger brother, the priest's two older sons—Jonathan and Simon—stepped up. They built a renewed army, taking up the name "Maccabee" in homage to Judah. They set about the work of reclaiming their country. Victory was achieved after they captured Jerusalem, sent the Seleucidians packing, and installed Jonathan as the high priest.

The Maccabees wanted Israel to govern itself, so they could worship and go about life under God's law. Unfortunately, the freedom purchased with the blood of the Maccabees was quickly squandered. In what would end up as Israel's last chance at sovereignty, the leaders stumbled.

Again.

Rather than embrace the system of self-governance God presented to Moses, they installed yet another human king. Divided loyalties arose, creating the "Pharisee" and "Sadducee" parties who competed—sometimes violently—for political leadership.

This created an opportunity for the region's new superpower, Rome, to step in. By 63 B.C., Israel had become a client kingdom. In 37 B.C., all pretense was dropped, and the Roman Senate installed Herod the Great as "King of the Jews."

Self-governance in Israel was destroyed by preening politicians more concerned with their own power and prestige than the principles of the people they nominally served.

Today's grassroots movement can relate. Remember those darlings of the Tea Party, elected officials whose heads were quickly turned by the establishment elite?

Think how often grassroots activists fight for candidates who, once in office, use the newfound political clout to ignore those who brought them to power. We see it with frustrating regularity. Rather than staying true to the principles upon which they campaigned, the politician betrays the grassroots and undermines his own legacy.

We must not allow the liberty achieved through self-governance to be sacrificed by politicians on the self-interested altars they erect to themselves. Even when elected officials become faithless, the citizenry must remain faithful to our principles.

The Maccabees failed to hold their movement and nation together. God's gift of self-governance vanished from Israel for two millennia. Let us pray we do better. Let us work to do better.

As citizens, the answer to all this is frustratingly simple: We must remain vigorously in the fight. It is up to us to remind the politicians that the political hammers used by the rabble to build their path to office can also be used to fight them out.

More importantly, we must remind ourselves that fight for liberty doesn't end when we elect "the right person"—it only intensifies. We must be fully and completely involved in the governing affairs of our cities, schools, counties, states, and nation.

That is the cost of citizenship in our Republic. That is the joy of citizenship in our Republic. That is the high calling of self-governance in our Republic.

BE A TROUBLER

False prophets only have sway with a people willing to be led astray.

False prophets tend to be popular; they tell us what we want to hear. Those who would expose false prophets find themselves served up as objects of derision, and as such must have the faith to persevere through withering criticism.

Each of us must be a thorn in the side of those who serve up a false god that happens to serve their interests. We must bring them trouble.

One of my favorite examples of causing trouble for the ruling elite plays out in the Old Testament Book of 1 Kings. The people had turned from God and began worshipping Baal. This is the "god" to whom worshippers sacrificed their small children in a horrifically vain attempt to appease that which was not there.

In 1 Kings 18, we find Elijah—the lone prophet of God at the time—derided as a "troubler" of Israel by the Baal worshippers. It was an apt title; the false prophets didn't like the trouble he was making for them by preaching about the true God.

As an aside, those false prophets didn't care about the people of Israel, they were serving themselves. By promoting the false teachings of Baal, they were accumulating power and wealth.

So at Mount Carmel a deal was struck. On one side would be 450 prophets of Baal, on the other was Elijah. Each would be calling on their respective god to light a fire. As one might imagine, the false prophets had no success, while the God of Elijah answered with a consuming blaze.

The false prophets were seized by a suddenly repentant people and slaughtered in the Kishon Valley. This fiery display of God's power brought the people of Israel back to Him, at least for a while.

And here's the rub: false prophets only have sway with a people willing to be led astray. The same is true today.

Think of the false prophets in our culture today, and the narratives they push from global warming to pandemic hysteria. Entire institutions exist to prop up the false prophets, and cancel those who would speak truth to their power.

Every crisis invented or promoted by the left has the exact same set of solutions: restrict travel, nationalize the economy, expand government, increase taxes. Whatever crisis they create, their "solutions" are always the same. And always come at the expense of liberty.

It is up to us to remain steady. We must keep our eyes fixed on God, on what is true even if unpopular.

When others fall under the self-induced spell of a false prophet, we must speak the truth even more loudly and boldly. Even if we must do so alone, we must be "troublers" to the unrighteous.

A JOYFUL RESPONSIBILITY
Preserving the Republic is your job.

A self-governing people must be eternally vigilant. The first three words of our Constitution make it clear who is supposed to be in charge: "We the people." Without the citizens taking an active and engaged role in civic life, the notion of self-governance collapses.

This has happened before. Will we let it happen again?

The Old Testament book of Second Samuel records how Israelites had grown tired of having God as their king and being responsible for living under His law. After demanding a human king like everyone else had, the Israelites quickly found the rule of man wasn't so much fun, either. The people of Israel saw their self-governing nation change for the worse—just as they had been warned.

After a period of foreign captivity and exile, God called His people back to Israel. A man named was Nehemiah was tasked with rebuilding the walls of Jerusalem, and in so doing restore the nation.

There were any number of enemies who wanted to thwart the return of the Jews, and so in Nehemiah 4:9, we're told that the people "prayed to our God and set a guard as a protection against them day and night." Everyone prayed, everyone worked, everyone guarded the work. Everyone was responsible.

They succeeded for a period, only to see their nation fall again. It is a cycle we should study, and seek to avoid.

If our nation conceived in liberty is to long endure, it will only be because we—the people—are wholly committed to being the Republic's self-governing leaders. We must each be actively engaged in the hard work of practical governance. We must be praying for each other and our countrymen. We must be prepared to defend our land. It is our duty, not someone else's.

We err when we allow ourselves to believe we can delegate the preservation of our Republic to someone else.

Rather, we must joyfully embrace the awesome responsibility of self-governance, so that we and our children can enjoy the fruits of Liberty. So let's resolve to pray, stay on guard, and get to work!

GIVING THANKS
Liberty is a necessary and integral component of our general prosperity.

We think we know the story of Thanksgiving: the pilgrims landed on Plymouth Rock, faced a harsh winter, famine and disease, and then only with the help of friendly natives learned how to survive. It's nice for bedtime stories, and feel-good paintings, but it ignores the most important lessons of our early history.

Let's clear up a myth. The pilgrims weren't city slickers. They didn't come to the New World ill-prepared for wilderness life, nor were they misguided about the challenges awaiting them. Sadly, the travails and trials of the pilgrims weren't the result of recklessness, ignorance, or chance.

No, the problems the pilgrims faced — and overcame — were of their very own making through a well-intentioned, though misguided, governing ideology.

William Bradford, the governor of Plymouth Colony, explains what happened in his *History of the Plymouth Settlement*. Even before arriving in the New World, they imposed on themselves what he called "communal service"—what we today would recognize as socialism.

Everything — the land, the work, the crops, everything — was held communally. Everyone was expected to work hard and receive only what they truly needed. As a result, Bradford wrote, many would simply "allege weakness and inability."

You won't be surprised that Bradford reported: "the young men who were most able and fit for service objected to being forced to spend their time and strength in working for other men's wives and children, without any recompense."

At the same time, "The strong man or the resourceful man had no more share of food, clothes, etc., than the weak man who was not able to do a quarter the other could."

Bradford would note: "Community of property was found to breed much confusion and discontent." No one had an incentive to work, so no one produced, and everyone was miserable.

Remember, this was a small group of people who shared common values, cared for each other, and had willingly joined philosophically to the colony's arrangements. It's just that socialism fails in practice whenever it is tried; sometimes it limps along, but ultimately the results are always the same.

Socialism—no matter what one calls it—always produces misery.

After three years, the colony abandoned its "communal" life. Bradford wrote that colony leaders divided the land among the families and "allowed each man to plant corn for his own household, and to trust to themselves for that."

As a result, Bradford added, "It made all hands very industrious, so that much more corn was planted than otherwise would have been by any means the Governor or any other could devise, and saved him a great deal of trouble, and gave far better satisfaction."

Private property rights and a free market carried the day. Labor was naturally divided – not politically imposed – and everyone utilized their skills to their own benefit, thereby increasing the productivity and happiness of the colony as a whole.

In the newly free society, where the local knowledge of Native Americans was combined with the techniques of Europe, the pilgrims had a harvest bountiful beyond comparison.

The very first days of the American experience demonstrated what world history repeatedly proves: socialism fails, and fails miserably. Bounty is produced by liberty driven by self-governance, not central planning – even when it is well intentioned.

We must remember that individual liberty is in the 21st century, as it was in the 17th, a necessary and integral component of our general prosperity. And let us be thankful to God daily not only for the material things we have but for the liberty of which He is the author.

CHEERFUL WARRIORS
The issues before us are deadly serious, but that doesn't mean we always have to be.

Due to the passage of time and cultural differences, we often miss the cutting and sometimes subversive humor employed in Scripture. That's unfortunate for many reasons, not the least of which is that a healthy dose of humor is a good way to combat a fallen world.

Now, let's be clear: Jesus wasn't a standup comedian, nor were the ancient prophets performers on "Whose Soul Is It Anyway?" Yet they were effective communicators and didn't shy away from employing that most dangerous of weapons: the wry chuckle.

The problem for us, as one author has put it, is that we in our very serious faith do not want to appear impious by laughing in the presence of the Divine. And then there is the practical challenge for us as modern readers of English Bibles translated from Greek, which—in Jesus' case—had themselves been translated from the spoken Aramaic. We don't catch the play on words, hear the lilt of the voice, or simply see the smile.

Everyone in earshot got the irony when Jesus said, after viewing a Roman coin bearing the image of the Roman emperor, "Render unto Caesar what is Caesar's and unto God what is God's." You can easily imagine Jesus smiling as he said this, and every Jew listening would have smiled along with Him. They all know this basic truth:

everyone, including Caesar, was made in God's image... and everything in creation belonged to God, even Caesar's coins. A nicely subversive dig at the ruling elite.

Jesus' cutting description of the ruling class as the blind leading the blind would have received a knowing laugh in an era not known for being particularly easy to navigate for the visually impaired. Often, He would sarcastically confront hypocritical religious leaders with the cutting phrase, "Have you not read?" since, of course, their claim to authority was their learned status.

Very often Jesus was saying out loud about the country's rulers what many quietly believed. He compared them to "vipers" and said it was easier for a camel to pass through the eye of a needle than for Jerusalem's political ruling class to make it into heaven.

On one of the occasions in which Jesus was about to be stoned by those rulers' sycophants, He not only kept his wits but employed them. He asked His would-be assailants, "I have shown you many good works from the Father. For which of these do you stone me?"

Yes, Jesus got angry—and with good reason. But more often than not, we find Jesus directing that righteous anger into loving action tinged with humor. He was the happy warrior in the battle for the souls of men.

What about you and me? There is no end to the litany of things about which to be angry—but it doesn't mean we have to be endlessly upset. The issues facing our Republic are deadly serious, but that doesn't mean we always have to be.

I understand why the other side is a grim lot, driven as they are by greed and envy. They are on the side of slavery and death. They know, deep in their hearts, that the best they can expect—if they are successful—is to be ruled over by tyrants who will destroy them last. *I'd be in a sour mood, too!*

We, however, should be of good cheer. As Ronald Reagan said, "We've made much progress already. So, let us go forth with good cheer and stout hearts—happy warriors out to seize back a country and a world to freedom."

In the eternal fight, our victory over death has been secured for us by Jesus. We're now the adopted sons and daughters of the Most High King. In this world, we get the honor of fighting to expand the promise of self-governance and extend liberty. We should do so with a smile on our face.

KEEP GOING

The fate of the Republic rests on the perseverance of patriots.

A few years back, my teenage son asked me to participate with him in a 5K race. I used to run for miles and miles and sprint 5Ks. Today, I can work up to an aggressive jog.

I knew what he was saying: "Dad, will you drive me to the race so I can speed past you, and then be eating doughnuts in the truck when you finally finish?"

So, of course, I agreed.

A quarter of the way through, my knee was bugging me. Then the other started.

Gotta keep going.

There was a lovely spot where it would have been nice to sit and rest, perhaps read for a bit.

Can't stop.

There were all these other people trudging along, too. One fellow had mentioned before the race it was his first time. A nearby lady's t-shirt proclaimed she was a cancer survivor.

How could I rest?

Discouragement, like a virus, spreads; it corrupts everything it touches.

I was reminded of the words of Paul in Hebrews 12, "And let us run with perseverance the race marked out for us."

The most important word there isn't "*run*"—it's "*perseverance.*"

We're called to persevere, to keep going. That's even more true in the fight for liberty than in that 5K. It's easy to be discouraged by the faithless and feckless politicians for whom we have spent time, energy, money, and sweat. It's easy to be pained by their unending capacity to capitulate against us.

It's okay to slow down, to change up the pace, to even walk a few steps. But it's not okay to give up. It's not acceptable to stop.

We must persevere. We must keep going, keep pursuing, never stopping. Not now, not ever.

The fate of the Republic rests on the perseverance of patriots. As Patrick Henry once proclaimed, "The battle, sir, is not to the strong alone; it is to the vigilant, the active, the brave." This American experiment in self-governance ends when the people give up.

A 5K ends after, well, five kilometers. The course of self-governance is never complete. To secure liberty and its blessings we must keep running, keep fighting, keep persevering.

LET THEM WHINE

Good governance requires the constant care and zealous vigilance of the citizenry.

When your opponents are complaining about how powerful you are, don't interrupt them. When the government cronies complain about your ability to frustrate their plans, let them keep talking. You are just doing your job as a citizen.

A donor told me he was increasing his giving to my organization because he had been to a meeting where some politicians were complaining about me. The politicians made it clear they didn't like my team exposing their records and self-serving antics.

"I figured if these powerful guys are so upset about your emails, tweets, and articles, then I want to be on your good side," he jokingly emailed me later.

His generosity was put to good use, reaching even more people. I did, however, have to remind him—if only for the sake of my own conscience—that those politicians who sneer, snicker, demean, and demagogue me aren't actually upset by what me and my team do. No, they are upset by the fact that citizens have a way to keep political score.

Despite their lofty rhetoric, politicians don't like an informed electorate. They don't like people asking pesky questions. They don't like taxpayers knowing the details of their backroom dealmaking.

Too bad!

Those seeking to undermine our Republic and erode liberty have never wanted witnesses to their dirty deeds. They encourage us to disengage from government; they pretend it is a virtue to be "apolitical." They promise to tell us what we need to know about what they have done to us, er, for us.

That is not how it is supposed to work.

Our system of government requires an informed and engaged citizenry. Unlike other nations, we were purposely formed as a self-governing Republic.

You and I don't have the constitutional right as citizens to put government on autopilot and expect only good things to happen. Good governance requires the constant care and zealous vigilance of the citizenry. It has always been that way. That is how our Republic was designed.

The most awesome and awe-inspiring appellation in our Republic is not president or governor, senator or councilman. You can search the world and not find a more sought-after or desired title than that of "citizen of the United States."

Our sacred duty as citizens, for each other and our posterity, is to help those around us be as informed and as engaged as possible. Yes, it will make the power-hungry, self-serving cronies whine. Let them whine: you have a Republic to save.

LIBERTY IS FRAGILE

Liberty only grows in the soil of self-governance tended by zealous patriots.

Liberty does not happen by accident. While we have an inalienable right to liberty, history demonstrates there is a big difference between securing it and holding on to it.

It would be nice to think "liberty" is the norm and "tyranny" is the exception. It would be nice, but it would not be true.

In the late 1940s, a businessman named Henning Prentis noticed a pattern in history. This pattern leads from bondage to liberty and back to bondage.

The so-called "Prentis Cycle" was developed in a series of speeches and essays. It goes like this:

> "From bondage to spiritual faith; from spiritual faith to courage; from courage to freedom; from freedom to abundance; from abundance to selfishness; from selfishness to complacency; from complacency to apathy; from apathy to fear; from fear to dependency; and from dependency back to bondage once more."

We like freedom and abundance, but in our selfishness and complacency we reject faith. We convince ourselves we have nothing to fear from the tyrant we shackle ourselves to under the promise of his benevolent protection. Anyone courageous enough to speak out is mocked and attacked.

Where are we today? Still in "abundance"? Shifted to "selfishness"? Moving past "fear"?

If we are to *reclaim* and *retain* liberty, we must renew our faith and shore up our courage. We must shake our friends out of their complacency and apathy.

Liberty can only grow in the soil of self-governance tended to daily by zealous patriots.

It isn't someone else's job. It is my job, and your job. It is a job for which we must actively train up our children. The cause of liberty never ends.

STICKS AND STONES

For better or worse, words reveal our heart as surely as our actions.

As rejoinders to bullies go, the old rhyme about "sticks and stones" being more physically harmful than words is true on its face, but fails the test of civil engagement for a self-governing people.

"Sticks and stones may break my bones, but words will never hurt me!" It's a chant often recited through barely-held-back tears. A more true rejoinder might be: "I'm rubber, you're glue; bounces off me and sticks on you."

After all, our words often say more about us than those at whom they are directed.

I thought about those rhymes while reading an excellent book by Rev. Eugene Peterson, "Answering God: The Psalms as Tools for Prayer." He begins by noting that the word "Torah"—the Jewish name for the first five books of what Christians know as the Old Testament—comes from the same root as the word for "javelin."

Peterson wrote, "In living speech, words are javelins hurled from one mind into another. The javelin word goes out of one person and pierces another."

In politics, it is easy to use words as javelins. Pointed adjectives hurled with powerful verbs can do a shocking amount of damage.

Oftentimes, words say more about the person speaking them than the target. Words reveal our heart as surely as our actions.

As a self-governing people, as the sovereigns in this Republic, we must always remember that our words carry great weight. We can and must be passionate about public policy; our Republic cannot afford the luxury of civic indifference.

Our Republic also cannot withstand citizens who take, and make, the actions of public officials as personal slights. If the mayor rams through a city council resolution declaring tomorrow "Joe Smith Should Be Shunned Day," then maybe ol' Joe can take it personally; for everyone else, the matter must be reviewed with an eye towards a corrective cleansing at the ballot-box.

If self-governance is to survive and thrive, we must be able to passionately and civilly discuss public policy in a way that directs our javelins in service of building the future we want. We must use our passions, ideas, words, sticks, and stones in the service of constructing a stronger Republic. In doing so, we will shine as a testament to the powerful gift of self-governance given to us by God.

WATCH YOUR LANGUAGE!
The words we use define our world and shape our actions.

The great military philosopher Sun Tzu warned his students not to let their enemies pick the time and location of battles. Sun Tzu wrote, "The clever combatant imposes his will on the enemy, but does not allow the enemy's will to be imposed on him."

When you fight on your enemies' terms, it rarely works out well.

You'd think this would be self-evident, but time and again conservatives let liberals define the fights. It is no wonder the war for our culture and Republic is in shambles!

Words matter; they shape how we view the world. For example, the Himba tribe from Namibia has no word for the color blue. When researchers showed them diagrams of 12 squares—11 green and one blue—the tribesmen didn't recognize the difference. As a jungle people, though, they saw huge differences in various shades of green that weren't completely obvious to the researchers.

Language, and how we use it, not only defines our world but shapes our actions.

Conservatives have all too often allowed themselves to be backed into a corner, losing battles for culture and government before the debate even begins.

This happens by adopting the language of the left. Conservative politicians will *say* they adopt the other side's definition of terms as a reasonable concession to civic dialogue. In fact, they do it often because they are intellectually insecure or emotionally lazy. Or, maybe, they are revealing their true beliefs.

On issue after issue, time after time, conservatives cede the selection of the rhetorical battleground to the left.

For example, we don't insist on using the language of life; instead, we capitulate by calling the infanticide brigade "pro-choice." When you define your opponents' position as "pro-choice," you set yourself up just a heartbeat away from losing.

I cringe when Republicans talk about government budgets "paying for" tax cuts. When one starts, as leftists do, with the presumption that government owns everything, then—perhaps—government decides how much you keep of what they say is their money in your bank account.

But as free-market conservatives, allegedly, we believe wealth is created by individuals. Governments have only what has been taken from citizens in the form of taxation.

People who enter a country without permission have long been known legally as illegal aliens; they do not belong where they are and have broken laws to enter. But the term "illegal aliens" became "illegal immigrants," and now that's morphed into "undocumented migrants." This was a purposeful transition of language.

Listen to speeches on the border crisis from your favorite conservative politicians, and notice how often they talk about the issue using words of the left. Then, think about why those politicians are having so little success in solving the issue.

They have allowed the opposition to define not just the issue but the terms under which the issue is debated.

They do this because they know that determines the scope of actions available and even how to establish success. How you approach the problem of "undocumented migrants" is vastly different than how you deal with "illegal aliens" or "invaders."

Language defines our world and shapes our actions. The real fight is never the fight itself; the real fight is for the terms and definitions around employed in the fight.

If conservatives want to be competitive in the war for culture and government, they must stop letting liberals pick the battlefields and define the terms. Conservatives cannot afford any longer to be bullied into using the left's manipulated language.

If conservatives are to be dominant in the war for our culture and government, they must be more disciplined in their language. More importantly, conservatives must impose on the national conversation the issues that matter most to them and define success as nothing less than saving our Republic.

THEY ARE NOT MAINSTREAM
Pretending the legacy media is "mainstream" only legitimizes the illegitimate.

You'll often hear people refer to the "mainstream" media, meaning the collection of leftist-controlled newspapers and television networks that once held sway over the dissemination of facts and opinions.

In fact, there is nothing "mainstream" about them.

As evidenced by their declining sales, diminishing market penetration, and vanishing economic viability, these legacy outlets are not mainstream. If the newspapers and networks that get so casually labeled "mainstream" actually were, they wouldn't be laying off staff while seeing their circulations and viewerships diminish.

Texas newspapers, for example, have fewer readers than ever before, despite the massive surge in population. They will snivel about "online" readership, but the paywalls they established haven't made any of them profitable. After all, no one wanted to read the drivel posing as online content when it was free...

Newspapers around the nation are dying precisely because they are not in the mainstream. You might be able to say they were once mainstream, but they are not anymore. The legacy media does not sit in the "mainstream" of political or cultural thought, but on the far-left bank.

Pretending they are "mainstream" is to legitimize the illegitimate.

Predictably, the dismal state of the media has caused handwringing about the downfall of democracy and other such blather. In fact, the rapid decline of the corporatist, crony establishment media might just be what saves our Republic.

Despite what a couple of generations of newspaper and TV network reporters claim, the First Amendment to the Constitution has absolutely nothing whatsoever to do with the flailing (and failing) corporate media. The First Amendment did not create a special class—what some self-righteously describe as the "Fourth Estate," as if it were some branch of government.

No, the First Amendment protects the right of the people, as individuals, to run printing presses, to publish, to speak, to broadcast. Every single one of us has the right to be the media, to be journalists.

Our Republic sprang to life in part because our Founding Fathers formed committees of correspondence in each of the colonies—subverting the loyalist media and keeping each other apprised of what was really happening in the colonies.

In the 21st century, citizens have stopped outsourcing their personal responsibility as journalists to the establishment hacks and are looking to each other for news, information, and opinions. It is driving the establishment berserk.

Technology has freed citizens from the tyranny of the establishment media, which is why the statists are seeking to place a stranglehold on actual mainstream voices in social media.

That means each of us must speak louder.

Someone is always keeping score in politics and government; I think it ought to be the citizens. That only happens when we know what is really going on. As a self-governing people, it is up to each of us to keep our neighbors, friends, and family informed and engaged—so we can together save the Republic.

STOP LAYING AROUND

Rather than be defined by anger, we must get to work fixing our Republic.

Scripture is full of paralyzed and lame individuals being healed, but one story has always stood out for me. That is because it seems so cruel.

On the surface, what Jesus said to a lame man lying near the Bethesda Pool in Jerusalem was mean. "Do you want to be healed?"

Let me back up. Myth had it that when the waters of the Bethesda Pool were disturbed by an angel, the first person to touch the water would be healed of their malady. Invalids—the blind, the paralyzed, and otherwise lame—would gather there in hopes of being the first one into the water.

So, yes, Jesus, *of course* the man wants to be healed. Except... we all know people who don't. We all know people who are comfortable in their misery, who find their life's meaning and worth wrapped up in suffering.

This man was different; he explained how he had no one to help him move into the water at the first ripple. He wanted to be healed but lacked anyone to help him. And so Jesus did, and it didn't involve dropping into the pool.

I see the same sort of thing repeated every day. I see people paralyzed by their anger over the state of our nation. They complain bitterly about the news of the day; they want someone to fix things.

To be sure, there is a lot to be angry about; but, when given the opportunity to learn how to make a difference, they sniff and look away. They define themselves by their anger, and they are—frankly—comfortable with just being mad.

Others, though, are tired of sitting on the couch. They are ready to redefine themselves not as passive recipients of bad news, but as agents of action. These are the people who make a difference in their communities, schools, states, and nation. They just need someone to show them how.

As an aside, Scripture tells us the man couldn't stop telling people what had been done for him. We don't know what else he did, but I suspect the man didn't slow down for the rest of his life, nor could he stop talking about how he had been healed, and by Whom.

What about us? Is it easier to stay on the couch and yell at the cable news shows? Or, are we willing to stop laying around? Are we ready to wake up our fellow citizens? Are we ready to zealously work for a better tomorrow? We can grouse about how bad things are, or we can grab the opportunity to make things better.

Our nation needs us to define ourselves not by our anger, but by our willingness to stand up and get to work.

THE COST OF BETRAYING OUR HERITAGE

Taxes are a reminder that we've made government our god.

Those who impose taxes are always quick to plead the righteousness of the levy, as though it were a divine sacrament. We're told we should feel some sort of patriotic zeal for bearing the burden of a bloated government that far exceeds its constitutional size.

When the ruling elite in Jerusalem tried to trip up Jesus and ask about the Roman tax burden, He famously deflected. "Render to Caesar the things that are Caesar's, and to God the things that are God's." Jesus knew they weren't really curious about tax policy; they just wanted an excuse to turn Him into a criminal.

Rather than Pharisees trying to trip us up, we have the federal tax code. While the English language Bible has less than 800,000 words, the federal tax code has close to 10 million—and growing.

When Christians question the heavy burden of taxes, someone will misquote Jesus' words as a divine order to shut up and pay up. Others will quote Supreme Court Justice Oliver Wendell Holmes Jr.'s dissent in the 1927 case of *Compañía General de Tabacos de Filipinas v Collector of Internal Revenue*. "Taxes are what we pay for civilized society," Holmes wrote.

Except, they are not. Taxes are blunt instruments used by the ruling elite to harass and manipulate the people while enriching themselves and their cronies.

Is that harsh? Well, maybe... But it's not a bad summary of what God told Samuel when the prophet relayed to the Almighty that His chosen people wanted a human king to lord over them. God, of course, wanted them to govern themselves under His law.

In 1 Samuel 8, we find God's warning: The king "will take the best of your fields and vineyards and olive groves and give them to his attendants. He will take a tenth of your grain and of your vintage and give it to his officials and attendants. Your male and female servants and the best of your cattle and donkeys he will take for his own use. He will take a tenth of your flocks, and you yourselves will become his slaves."

Taxes are the "tithe" progressives impose on everyone in the name of their secular religion. This is why study after study shows progressives are not actually charitable with their own money; they conflate the imposition of taxes with actual charity.

Yes, yes, render unto Caesar... except that in our Republic the law is king and the citizens, not the politicians, are the sovereigns. As citizens, we have allowed a 10-million-word tax code to be imposed upon us for the same foolish (and even sinful) reasons the people of Israel chose a king over God three millennia ago.

Modern taxation is not the price of civilized society; it is the cost of betraying our heritage of self-governance. If we want to reduce our tax burden, we must increase our civic activism.

BEING TRUSTWORTHY
Facts presented out of context create a lie.

In the economy of civics, "trust" is the only currency that counts. We all know that a flat-out lie is wrong, yet we tolerate the "shading" of truth when it serves our political purposes. It is so easy to pull honest-to-goodness facts out of their context to further our own ends.

Every parent has had this experience. A child is caught eating a snack right before dinner, so you ask, "Why are you spoiling your meal?" The child replies, "Mom said I could." The child isn't exactly lying; mom indeed had said the kid could have a snack... three hours earlier.

Scripture is replete with condemnations of lying. Proverbs 12:33 tells us "Lying lips are an abomination to the Lord, but those who act faithfully are his delight."

And let us not forget that most awkward of the Ten Commandments. To be clear: the Ninth Commandment doesn't say, "Don't lie," which is how we try to explain it. True enough, but this explanation misses the mark through simplification.

Instead, God tells us to "not bear false witness against your neighbor." This covers a lot more waterfront than just "do not tell a lie." It goes to the heart of what we say, what we communicate, and what we are attempting to make our neighbor hear.

This is where context matters. Facts, when presented out of context, will create a lie.

We see this all the time in politics.

Not long ago we were treated to the spectacle of a Republican lawmaker bragging in a special election about how he was a proponent of a popular GOP reform. In fact, he was responsible for the measure being watered down to the point of being useless. After the bill was gutted, he then voted for it. So when he told his constituents he supported the measure, he was telling the truth way outside the context of what he had actually done.

As Martin Luther put it, "You are not only responsible for what you say, but also for what you do not say."

As an aside, this is part of why Americans have grown weary of the legacy media. Rather than report facts in their correct context, many legacy reporters and newscasters lie through manipulative editing and careful omission.

Our system of self-governance demands that we tell each other the truth, using facts in context. It isn't always convenient to the establishment politicians, their apologists in the media, or paymasters in the lobby, but it is critical to the high calling of citizenship.

YOU DON'T NEED A PLAN
It is up to the public servants to get the citizens' business done.

No demand against the citizens is quite so cutting as when a politician, after being chastised for inaction, replies, "Ok, fine. What's your plan?" It is a retort designed to render critics mute, but it is a reminder that our public servants are anything but.

The "what's your plan" retort from politicians is evidence that we have all lost our way. They strut around with it as their rhetorical weapon of choice. Whenever it is aimed by a politician or a politician's sycophantic supporters, I see citizens pushed back on their heels.

The question's potency arises from its simplicity. We are taught as children by our parents not to have a complaint for which we don't have a solution. In business, we are told to present our boss with a plan, not a problem.

But in the world of government policy, the citizens are neither children nor employees—and the officeholders are not our parents or bosses. Or, at least, that is how our system was designed.

We have allowed the governing roles to be flipped upside-down. We have allowed politicians to set themselves up as the nation's masters. We have allowed elected officials to see themselves as our betters, as the American nobility, as the dispenser of rights. We let them define us dismissively as the masses.

In our self-governing Republic, the highest title in a particular jurisdiction is not president, governor, or mayor, but citizen. The citizens are the politicians' employers. The citizens are the guardians of the Republic.

The politicians are supposed to be the servants.

Throughout history, the master-servant model has been well understood. The master must merely have a goal in mind; it is the servant's job to make it happen. The head of the house doesn't need to know the mundane details of the kitchen operations when demanding that dinner be served promptly at seven o'clock. It is up to the servant to make it happen or suffer the consequences.

There is no "partnership" between a master and a servant. Citizens are not in partnership with politicians. Politicians in our Republic exist to implement the agenda set by the citizens in keeping with the limitations of the Constitution.

As a citizen, you have no obligation to come up with the detailed operational plans for reducing taxes or whatever other policy goal you have in mind. If you want to, that's great—but it's not required and shouldn't be expected. The men and women who stand before the body politic and declare themselves mentally and morally fit to solve the problems identified by the citizens must, once hired, get to work—not make self-serving excuses for inaction.

Those politicians who demand that you give them a plan for an issue are telling you they only want the title, not the work. Your responsibility as a citizen is to set expectations for the public servants. It is their job to deliver.

Citizens must impose an agenda on politicians, and then hold those public servants accountable for achieving it.

THE ARMY YOU NEED
God's tactics are anything but conventional.

It has been said that you go to war with the army you have, not necessarily the army you think you need or want. In the battles of everyday life, we can always point to the things we don't have that would make life easier.

But would they?

As a self-governing people, we must learn to see the value in what we have—in what has been provided for us—and move forward in faith.

One of my favorite examples of this is found in the sixth and seventh chapters of Judges. We read how the people of God were preparing to attack their enemies; the Israeli force was 20,000 strong against an even larger opponent. But, still, it was an impressive force that had been assembled by the Israelites' military leader, Gideon.

Gideon had faith the Israelites would achieve victory, but he had to see that it would be on God's terms.

Even today, you can travel to the spring where God had Gideon winnow the troops in what might be one of the more unconventional military tactics in the Bible (and, let's face it, the Bible is full of them).

First, God told Gideon to let anyone leave who was fearful of taking on a powerful army. Half did so. Then, He instructed Gideon: "Every one who laps the water with his tongue, as a dog laps, you shall set by himself. Likewise, every one who kneels down to drink."

There were just 300 who lapped the water; God wanted them. The rest were sent packing. (As a quick aside: Would you want to be with those uncouth water-lappers? It is a reminder that God's army usually isn't what we'd expect.)

It is no secret why God did this; He was abundantly clear. God said He did not want Israel to "boast over me, saying, 'My own hand has saved me.'" God wanted Gideon and all of Israel to understand their victory was His working, not theirs.

In the polity of God, He is the unified majority. As was demonstrated at Gideon's spring, an army of thousands can be routed by 300. Except God wants the 300, and their beneficiaries, to understand the true source of the victory.

As we go about our daily struggles and battles, God has given us all we need to be successful and victorious. We must simply proceed faithfully with the allies and tools God has provided, knowing victory will come in His time.

PRAYING FOR THE WRONG PEOPLE

Stop acting, and praying, like a serf; you are the ruler.

Are we praying for the wrong people? In a word: yes.

I hear this segment of a prayer all the time: Someone will have asked the audience to bow our heads and join them in praying. At some point—particularly at church or a political gathering—will come the inevitable: "And now we pray for our leaders," followed by a list of well-known names or public offices.

The particularly pious, hoping to evoke a sense of biblical weight, will prayerfully refer to the president, governor, or mayor as our "rulers."

It reminds me just how ignorant we have become in our Republic, just how far we have devolved in our understanding of how government is supposed to work. We don't elect "rulers" or "leaders" here; we elect servants.

So let me say it again: Every time you hear someone pray for our nation's "rulers" and "leaders" to have wisdom in addressing the issues of the day, they are praying—ultimately—for the wrong people if the focus is on the politicians.

We should pray not as submissive serfs under the heavy thumb of feudal lords, but as kings earnestly seeking divine guidance for ourselves and our fellow regents. We, the people, are the leaders.

Now, don't get me wrong: We absolutely must pray for the public servants holding these specific positions—just like an employer should pray feverishly for her employees, or a commander for the soldiers under his command.

All too often, though, the real leaders in our system of government, the ones for whom those title-holders work and take orders, never seem to be the object of corporate prayer. The citizenry has become an afterthought—if ever thought of at all—even by the citizens.

Yes, an ancient kingdom's fortunes shifted with the attitude of the king, and Rome became a Christian empire because of Emperor Constantine's edict. But in our Republic, the citizen is the ruler.

All of this is by design; our Founding Fathers rejected kings and bequeathed us a constitutional Republic where the direction is driven by the citizens. Don't like where the country is heading? The problem starts not at the White House, but in our neighborhoods.

It is very easy, in a fallen world, to want a single person on whom we can thrust blame and outsource responsibility. The people of Israel certainly did so when they rejected the system of self-governance under God and demanded a human king. Just as the ancient Israelites suffered for abandoning the political system designed for them by God, our abdication of governing obligations undergirds many of our modern political problems.

It is you, me, and our fellow citizens who rule; we are the "governing authorities" described in Romans 13—not someone else. Even absentee citizens, those who don't bother to participate, are still ruling—they are just ruling very badly.

The responsibility to govern the Republic wisely rests with us. As for those who want to be ruled over as subjects rather than bearing the moral responsibility of being the ruler? They should find somewhere else to live.

Praying for our Republic's politicians and not the citizens is like asking a physician to alleviate the symptoms without addressing the disease. If we want righteous men and women to hold public office, we must start by praying for our neighbors and countrymen to be consumed by a desire for righteousness.

Yes, we should pray for our public servants, for the men and women holding public office, but we should pray harder for our fellow citizens. If we are praying for the hearts of our nation's leaders to be inclined to God, we must be praying more often—and much more explicitly—for the hearts and attitudes of our fellow citizens.

ACCESS FOR WHAT?

Stop worshipping at the altar of political access.

No private sin is quite so publicly ensnaring as the quiet promise of political access. It trips up the most sure-footed activist and silences even the boldest advocate of liberty.

The fourth chapter of Mathew's Gospel records the specific temptations dangled in front of Jesus by Satan. I categorize them as pairings of comfort and ease, safety and power, and vanity and prestige.

For example, we read that Jesus was taken to a "very high mountain" where Satan showed Him "all the kingdoms of the world and their glory." It was there Satan said, "All these I will give you, if you fall down and worship me."

Jesus immediately responded, "Be gone, Satan! For it is written, 'You shall worship the Lord your God and him only shall you serve.'"

Too many in politics—politicians and citizens alike—have taken the deal Jesus rejected. They justify doing so with a recitation of all the alleged "good" they could theoretically achieve.

I have elected officials constantly tell me they must make compromises with the devil—a phrase they themselves employ without irony—so they can "do good things." I bet Jesus could have justified saying "yes" just like that. I know I could; I've heard variations of it an uncountable number of times.

And it's not just the politicians.

Not long ago a well-known Christian conservative told me he was going against his base of supporters—and even "sacrificing" his own conscience—by endorsing a corrupt legislators in the corps of cronies, despite a viable challenger. He claimed by taking such an action he would demonstrate an ability to maintain relationships with elected officials. His rationale? So he could be an insider, and therefore get good things done down the road.

Once one starts worshiping at the altar of political access, those "good things" used as the initial justification happen less and less. Can't lose that access! And, in their final evolution, the agreeable access-seeker is found to be working against the principles he once so loudly espoused.

Like any addictive substance, satisfying the need for access becomes an all-consuming need to which anything will be sacrificed.

Over the years, a sad number of activists have become addicted to the access afforded to them by being friendly with those in power. Rather than risk alienation, they move from citizen-leader to political-sycophant. Where they once boldly spoke truth to power, they end up defending governing malfeasance.

This is why Jesus said "no" to the devil's bargain. He knew He had access to a power far greater than earthly princes. He knew where such a compromise would lead.

The same is even more true for each of us. The access we should crave is to God, not the powers and principalities of the world.

As citizens in a self-governing Republic, we must reject the "access" model of politics. Instead, we must hold each other accountable by speaking honestly in the face of governing temptation. By operating as a community of citizens, we can begin to reclaim our government.

PART III
OVERSEEING POLITICIANS

"What country can preserve its liberties if their rulers are not warned from time to time that their people preserve the spirit of resistance?"

– Thomas Jefferson

"Politics ought to be the part-time profession of every citizen who would protect the rights and privileges of free people and who would preserve what is good and fruitful in our national heritage."

– Dwight D. Eisenhower

STOP MAKING THEIR EXCUSES
Our relationship with politicians should be anything but personal.

When starstruck teenagers pines over the latest Hollywood manufactured heartthrob, excusing all manner of bad behaviors and looking for the barest of redemptive qualities, we laugh in the knowledge that such behavior will pass. Yet when it is an adult whose infatuation isn't with a singer or actor, but a politician, the look is a little less winsome. And a lot more worrisome.

No matter what they say, politicians want us to make politics intensely personal. They want us to think that they think of us all the time; they want us to feel a special bond with their family; they want us to feel like we're in a relationship with them.

Not unlike the talented crooner who convinces every pre-teen girl who buys his latest song that it was, secretly, written for her.

Politicians want us to feel an emotional loyalty to them unconnected to their job performance. They want us to not only excuse their bad behavior, but to actively defend the indefensible.

Our relationship with politicians should be anything but personal. While we should feel personal disgust at the state of our Republic, and sense a deeply personal urge to pursue good public policy, that is not the same as being sycophantic cheerleaders—or obedient serfs—for the politicians who temporarily hold positions of power.

All too often, I find people professing deep concern for an issue or cause, but nonetheless bend over backwards in defense of politicians who have done nothing more than pay them the barest lip service.

Here's my rule: If someone is making excuses for politicians, they are a subject and not a citizen; they are an apologist, not an activist.

I understand the urge to "maintain a relationship" with a politician. There is something to be said for being friendly with the hired help. But there is a big difference between not wanting the sorry excuse for a waiter spitting in your food, and demanding that your fellow patrons' all tip him extravagantly as you walk out the door.

As citizens, we must stop tolerating politicians who tickle our ears but refuse to fight for the values and principles we hold dear. Rather than make excuses for them, we should denounce them as frauds and find someone better.

In our Republic, the citizens—not the politicians—rule supreme. We must not fawn over them like love-sick teenagers, but rather demand they perform to our expectations.

WHO ARE THE IDIOTS?
Hint: We all need to look in the mirror.

Mark Twain didn't like school boards. He spoke often and disparagingly of them. At one point he wrote, "In the first place, God made idiots. That was for practice. Then he made school boards."

Why are school boards the pinnacle of idiotic behavior? The answer may not be what any of us want to hear.

Ours is a self-governing Republic. We don't elect masters, but servants. Our system only works when the citizenry holds elected officials and bureaucrats in careful check.

When an employer hires an employee who steals from the cash register and scares off the customers, the employer is at fault if he doesn't fire the miscreant. The behavior an employer tolerates will be the standard the rest of the employees follow.

The same goes for elections.

So let's think about that Mark Twain quote. One must ask: why are school boards filled with 'idiots'?

The uncomfortable answer? Voters have allowed it. It is our fault.

Self-governance as a governing model begins by governing ourselves.

In Texas, more than 90 percent of voters don't vote in school elections. Even fewer ask the necessary questions that would provide the kind of civic oversight required in our system of government.

If we're not doing our job as citizens, how can we expect the elected servants to do theirs? Or, to borrow Mark Twain's words: if the citizens act like idiots, why shouldn't the politicians?

Most everyone complains about multi-gazillion-dollar high school football stadiums... but then we don't vote in the elections where those decisions are decided.

From teacher quality to curriculum, no question in public governance can be asked that doesn't wind its way back to the public's lack of attention.

The answer to why school boards seem to engage so regularly in idiotic behavior... is found uncomfortably in the mirror.

So while school boards might be, as Twain alleged, the pinnacle of idiotic behavior, the fault rests with citizens who allow it.

If we want to stop the idiots, we ourselves must first stop being the idiots. School boards, and therefore the schools, will improve when the citizens are more engaged.

WHEN SOMEONE TELLS YOU WHO THEY ARE...
Believe them.

We should always assume the best about people; in many ways, it is what allows civil society to function. Life is easier when I assume the teller at the bank isn't secretly pocketing my cash when I make a deposit! I don't need to go looking for trouble, as the old adage goes.

Sometimes, though, individuals tell us who they really are. When they do, we really should believe them.

There is an unfortunate trend in politics for voters not to believe who their incumbents really are. For better or worse, candidates are essentially products. Marketing blitzes with carefully scripted ads, right down to perfectly poised family Christmas cards, create a sense of personal intimacy without actual substance.

We don't know them. We don't know the person; so we vote for the product.

But that product is a big-ticket item; like a house or a car. Yet more so, because our vote is an investment in the future of ourselves, our children, and our neighbors. We want to get it right.

Then the candidate becomes the officeholder who doesn't deliver. They prove themselves not to be the "fighter" portrayed in the ads, but another cog in the wheel of the establishment cronies. Sure, we dislike Congress—

but we really like our own congressman; he's the exception ... just like everyone else's congressman.

As you might imagine, no one ever campaigns for office as "cog for the cronies." Yet they show us that by their actions.

Enter the cognitive dissonance, that disquieting realization that comes when confronted with two things that cannot be true at the same time. The candidate cannot be both the "fighter" and the "lackey." If "all of Congress is bad," what are the chances that mine is the exception?

Here is the elegant solution used by frail egos. We made the decision to purchase that big-ticket item ... We made that promise to protect our kids ... We told our neighbors to embrace this person ... So we clam up. We willfully disbelieve the evidence in front of us.

The power of incumbency isn't the money or perks, but because we shackle ourselves to our own bad decisions. We shackle ourselves to the servant we hired on the basis of a fraudulent campaign.

We don't want to admit we were wrong, so we lash out at those who point to any inconvenient facts. We will even distort reality to match the outcome we wished had been achieved by our vote.

When it is a car, we say things like, "I think it is great that the back windows don't roll down and steering column doesn't adjust—fewer things that can go wrong!" When it is a politician, all too often we become fawning cheerleaders.

As the hiring officers on the committee to save the Republic, we should be something more than unpaid apologists. Citizens should treat the selection of our servants as less than a personal investment and more of a professional exercise. Rather than pridefully allow our losses to mount, we should be willing to move on.

When politicians show us who they really are, we should believe them, fire them, and then find someone who will actually deliver the outcomes we desire.

STOP BEING NICE

We can be nice serfs, or we can be driven citizen-leaders.

Most of us live our days striving to be nice. We think we can just be all smiles and exude love by being nice to those who do evil. It's a niceness that doesn't appear in Scripture, and achieves only a self-serving sense of righteousness.

In Scripture, we don't find this modern version of "nice" that so many secularists (and even church leaders) push Christians to embrace. We find love. We find generosity. We find kindness. We find sincerity. We find patience.

But this gooey, saccharine-sweet niceness is nowhere to be found.

On nearly every page of the Gospels, you find Jesus dining with culture's untouchables, healing the infirm, instructing the weak. But He isn't "nice"; he is firm, honest, patient, holy. He tells them the truth about their sin. He tells them to "go and sin no more."

But with the ruling elite of the day? With the rulers who profit from self-dealing and cronyism? He calls them "serpents" and a "brood of vipers." He says they are "whitewashed tombs." He calls them murderers. These words weren't directed at the occupying Romans, or the atheists, or adherents to other religions; they were pointed at His fellow Jews.

Nothing about that was "nice." It was true. It was honest. And it was a kindness to those who were being oppressed.

No doubt many wanted Jesus to just be nice. You can hear them demand, "More of the 'water into wine' and 'free bread and fish,' Jesus, and less of the viper-talk."

It is no different today. I can only speak to the experience of Republicans, but those who yell the loudest for citizens to be "nice" to politicians are the ones profiting off selling out the values and principles for which the GOP reportedly stands.

We can be nice serfs, or we can be driven citizen-leaders. We can smile pleasantly as our Republic is run into ruin, or we can fight for the inheritance of self-governance meant for ourselves and our posterity.

Rather than be "nice," let us first and always strive to be passionate citizens faithfully committed to the cause of liberty.

WHO DO YOU SERVE?
It's not a trick question.

No question causes more discomfort than this: "Who do you serve?" Not long ago, I asked that question to a politician who bristled with indignation and replied, "I serve no one!"

His answer told me more than he knew.

If we cannot acknowledge who we serve, we cannot possibly build them up or serve them well. And I'm not talking in some deep, theological sense of serving God. I mean this literally: Who do you serve?

Two of my favorite books of the Old Testament are Joshua and Nehemiah. Both present great case studies in practical leadership. Undergirding both stories is the question of "who do you serve?" In Joshua, that question is explicit; in Nehemiah, it is implicit. Yet the answer is equally consistent: we must all live lives of service to each other.

I am reminded of that Roman Centurion in the Gospel of Matthew, a man of great power, who correctly told Jesus that everyone is under authority—even that politician I mentioned.

The politician wanted me to know he served no one, which meant he served himself. The correct answer would have been that he served the people, but I would still have had a little more respect for him if he had named off a crony lobbyist or two. Instead, all I saw was a man deluded by his appreciation for his (temporary) power.

In a Republic established under the principles of self-governance—where the law, not a man, is king—we are each in the curious position of being each other's masters and servants.

But no title in our nation is more exalted than that of "citizen." Every "honorable" person with a fancy government title is merely one of the servants. The people are in charge; the people are the masters.

Or, rather, they are supposed to be.

We must remind those in office that they answer to us, and not the other way around. We should remind ourselves of that as well. As citizens, we must stop idolizing elected officials and instead take an active role in leading our communities.

We all serve someone. Yes, we must serve God—but we serve Him in large part by serving each other. As a self-governing people, serving each other is a critical component of our civic life. We must be daily about the business of building each other up as the real leaders our Republic needs us to be.

MAKE THEM FEAR YOU
We've allowed the politicians to think they are the masters of our Republic.

Fear is a powerful tool. Improperly applied, fear causes us to make irrational choices without thinking. Yet it can also, in the words of the Book of Proverbs, be the "beginning of wisdom." The difference is what we fear.

In Proverbs 9:10 we find, "fear of the LORD is the beginning of wisdom." Scripture is replete with examples of the foolishness of man. Individuals, prophets, and even disciples often make the mistake of fearing men more than God.

A healthy fear is critical in all facets of life. And, frankly, it is very easy to fear the wrong things.

I have come to believe what underlies many of our problems in the American body politic is too little fear. That is, too little fear by the politicians of the voters and taxpayers.

Were this not so, for example, we would not be treated to the routine spectacle of politicians tripping over themselves to get the taxpayers' cash to their cronies.

The fault rests with us.

What we should have been fearing is what has resulted. We should have feared the loss of liberty. We should have feared the growing bureaucratic deep-state. We should have used that fear to drive actions protecting our Republic.

But it was easier for us to fear the loss of free time that comes with being engaged. It was easier to fear the inconvenience of true self-governance.

We have allowed ourselves to fear the disapproval of power-hungry, self-serving politicians. We have feared being targeted by unelected bureaucrats. We have feared the disapproval of those who hate us.

And so, we have found ourselves fearing a government that—in our laziness—has become a prowling leviathan.

As citizens, we have failed to inspire sufficient fear in those elected servants. We've allowed them to think they are the masters of this Republic. We have put ourselves at the bottom of the governing hierarchy.

Too many citizens fail to even participate in elections. And even fewer bother to take the steps necessary to hold politicians accountable for their actions and inactions. The downward spiral of cause and effect blur, with the result being lawmakers who don't sufficiently fear the citizenry and citizens too fearful to engage effectively.

Wisdom is found in learning from our mistakes and being fearful of repeating them. Will we let fear stop us from fighting back?

It's up to us, as citizens, to inspire in our elected servants greater fear than the lobbyists and bureaucrats. Rather than accept table scraps, the citizenry must unwaveringly demand that politicians seek our approval and our approval alone.

As citizens, we must stand firm, and demand obedience from our government.

ACTION BEATS RHETORIC
A little less talking, a lot more doing.

George Washington rarely made speeches. Abraham Lincoln's most famous address ran just 271 words. Teddy Roosevelt famously said you should speak softly but carry a big stick. Whatever else one thinks of them, they were men who let their actions speak louder than their words.

Unfortunately, too many politicians in the modern era put talk ahead of action. They want applause for their words, without suffering the indignity of working to make them real. Too many in elected office want to be judged by what they have said, rather than what they have substantively accomplished.

Modern politicians seem to have an almost pathological compulsion to resist delivering on their promises.

Our Republic could do with a little less talking and a lot more doing. Citizens and taxpayers have been demanding important reforms for years. Politicians pay lip service to the ideas when campaigning, but rarely seem to find the time to actually get them done.

As an aside, that might be why Donald Trump was so hated by so many in the political establishment. Yes, he talked a lot. Yes, his words were sometimes poorly considered or ill-timed. And yet, he got a lot done.

The Apostle James wrote, "What good is it, my brothers, if someone says he has faith but does not have works? Can that faith save him?"

James, of course, was writing about a faith that isn't backed up by matching actions. I once had a pastor say he could hear someone profess what they believe, or he could look at their calendar and checkbook and know for certain.

His point, of course, was that talk is cheap, but how we spend our time and money—our actions—will show our true heart.

The same is true in politics. What good are politicians' promises to do good, when they don't actually do it?

Citizens in our self-governing Republic should be less interested in what our public servants say and more focused on what they do... or fail to do. A politician can tickle our ears all day long with promises to do our bidding, but the proof of their commitment to liberty is found in what they actually accomplish.

CONFUSING VOLUME AND MASS
Being loud isn't the same thing as being effective.

It's easy to confuse volume with mass in politics. Our inboxes, social media feeds, news shows ... everything is set to maximum screech. All of which makes it hard for citizens to the discern the substance of issues.

My grandfather once passed on something he'd heard from a mounted cavalry sergeant. This was back in the waning days of the "ride horses" U.S. Army into which my grandfather had enlisted. The sergeant said that if out in the distance you saw a wall of dust climbing into the sky, it could be one of three things: an invading army, an approaching storm, or an idiot running around in circles. To know what to do, you had to know which it was.

That came to mind when a friend recently wrote asking about a particular candidate in a particular race. She explained she was receiving multiple emails every day from the candidate about the strength of the campaign, yet was shocked when she saw how little money the candidate had raised. More so, she found no evidence that the candidate had any footing in the community. What she saw didn't match the flood of emails, tweets, and posts she saw every day.

She asked a simple question: why the disparity?

A teeny-tiny Bluetooth speaker can make a lot of earsplitting noise, while a ton of gold will fill a pick up truck's bed but makes no sound. Volume and mass.

In the physics of politics, volume often creates mass ... Run around in circles, make a lot of noise, and hope others join in. That is campaigning 101 in the modern age, and that's kind of what the campaign my friend wrote about was trying to achieve.

Depending on your perspective, the campaign was either trying to convert political volume into a mass of support through messaging, or was using the volume of messaging to conceal their lack of mass.

Either way, citizens should be wary of those politicians who are simply running around in circles, creating a big cloud of dust while yelling and screaming their own praises. That self-serving exercise gives a sense of how they will govern if given the chance.

Campaigns try to give the appearance of mass with the volume of communication, in the hopes of drawing more people in. It works more often than anyone would care to admit. One gets the uncomfortable feeling too many candidates would wear clown make-up and shoot themselves from a loud cannon if it would get them a few more votes. One gets the even more uncomfortable feeling it would probably work. (As an aside, those candidates will often perform for the voters, wash off the makeup, and then brag to lobbyists about how they—again—pulled one over on the rubes.)

In our self-governing Republic, citizens should demand something more and better. Sure, a bit of showmanship and a touch of volume is necessary to cut through the clutter. But citizens deserve to see real results, not choke on distracting clouds of campaign dust.

For our Republic to advance, we must demand substantive candidates offering real plans for how they will disrupt the status quo. We need a mass of moral men and women seeking office who are committed to putting our citizens first.

More importantly, though, as discerning citizens we must ignore the self-serving circus of political gamesmanship and redouble our focus on the "mass" of good ideas—shaping them, moving them, and advancing them.

WHAT WE TRUST IN

Too many people cast their hopes and fears on the personalities of politicians.

Since 1956 the official motto of the United States of America has been "In God We Trust," and the phrase has appeared on our currency since the mid-1860s.

What do you believe in? What do we believe in?

It surprised me to realize one of my favorite stops in Israel was the archeological tel known popularly as Ancient Shiloh. It is the very spot where the Tabernacle of God stood for more than 350 years before moving to Jerusalem. It is the spot where Hannah brought her son Samuel and dedicated him to the service of God.

It is where the people later came to Samuel. It is where they rejected the system of self-governance God had given them and demanded the establishment of a monarchy —despite severe warnings from God Himself.

The people of God decided, as you can read in 1 Samuel 8, to put their trust in a big, secular, man-devised government. We've been making the same mistake ever since.

In so many real and practical ways, all of Western civilization's governing mistakes and missteps are traced to that rejection of God's practical provision of self-governance.

Those warnings from God came to fruition over the next several decades for those people at that time, and those problems have been with us ever since. There is never any profit to be found in trading out God's wisdom for the baubles of the world.

The Psalmist—who was very likely Israel's second king, David—grappled with being a king as surely as he grappled with his own painful awareness of his inadequacy and sin. He knew his kingdom would fade, but that God's would last forever.

In Psalm 146:3-7 we find:

"Put not your trust in princes, in a son of man, in whom there is no salvation. When his breath departs, he returns to the earth; on that very day his plans perish. Blessed is he whose help is the God of Jacob, whose hope is in the LORD his God, who made heaven and earth, the sea, and all that is in them, who keeps faith forever; who executes justice for the oppressed, who gives food to the hungry."

There is truly nothing new under the sun, as David's son Solomon would later write. Then, as now, we find too many people casting their hopes and fears on the personalities of politicians, rather than the eternal God of Abraham, Isaac, and Jacob.

True justice is found with the Creator of the universe, not self-serving politicians.

Just as we cannot trust government agencies to save us, neither can we outsource our governing responsibilities to corruptible politicians. To protect our public servants from corruption, we must limit the fearsome power available to them. That, too, was wrapped up in the practical wisdom of God's design for self-governance that His people rejected.

Our Founding Fathers believed that strictly limiting the size and scope of the government was a design feature of our Republic; our generation has treated it as a flaw.

The God who made us in His image calls us to be a self-governing people. That starts by trusting in Him not just with our words, but by our actions.

POLITICAL CORRUPTION IS OUR FAULT

It only ends when we remember who is in charge.

When public corruption by government officials is alleged, everyone typically rushes to partisan corners—either in defense of their allies or to chastise opponents. No one will admit someone from their political team might have fallen prey to the seduction of power, and we assume our opponents live exclusively on the wrong side of the ethical divide.

We should all take a deep breath.

As citizens in this Republic, we must expect better of our public servants. More importantly, we must demand better of ourselves.

Take, for example, a store owner whose employees are cheating customers and making side deals with vendors. If the store owner allows the activity to continue, their error becomes his. He certainly won't get much sympathy when those employees start stealing from the cash register. The collapse of the business is his fault, for the simple fact that he tolerated the culture leading to its demise.

The same is true in our Republic.

No response to an allegation (or confirmation) of public corruption is more disgusting, however, than when people just shrug and excuse it as "how things are." That is a sorry indictment of us, because it presumes someone else is in charge.

As a self-governing people, we are, in fact, the ones in charge. We are responsible for setting the moral environment in which our public servants work. While the store owner I mentioned could just close his business, our practical duties and moral responsibilities as citizens are not so easily dissolved.

In the third chapter of Romans, we're reminded of a simple human truth: "All have sinned and fall short of the glory of God." All of us are sinners, and so we sin. Every one of us, when given enough power, will abuse it for our own ends.

Or, as Lord Acton put it, "Power corrupts, and absolute power corrupts absolutely."

This lesson pervades the pages of the Bible and history. The first king of Israel, Saul; his successor, David; and even the wisest king, Solomon, were testaments to this truth.

It is why our Founding Fathers sought to replicate the biblical system of self-governance—which the people of Israel had rejected, giving rise to the corruption of their kings. Our Founding Fathers envisioned a highly decentralized government, built around checks on power, to preserve liberty and limit corruption.

Yet like the ancient Israelites, we have tolerated the unbalancing of those checks, even cheering as government power has been concentrated and grown beyond the constitutional framework. Then we feign surprise when this power is abused and officials are found to have engaged in self-dealing activities.

Shame on us for offloading our responsibilities as citizen-leaders to the hired help. Shame on us for feeding the culture of corruption by making the servants more than they are, and enticing them with power to abuse in service to themselves. Shame on us for turning elected officials into idols.

We must not tolerate public corruption under the belief "our man wouldn't do this" or "at least it's not the other party in charge" or even because "this is how things are."

No; public corruption is a disease in the body politic that we have allowed to fester. It ends only when we demand better of our public servants, and of ourselves.

DON'T GET DISTRACTED

For too long, too many of us have been lulled to civic sleep or pointed in the wrong direction.

A friend recently attended a meeting of the Texas Republican Party's state executive committee meeting. On the docket was a proposal for communicating publicly what the GOP grassroots expected the state's GOP-dominated House and Senate to deliver in the coming legislative session. A sniveling apologist for the lawmakers fretted that the elected officials wouldn't like being told what to do.

Too bad.

Our Republic was not designed for the convenience of a special elite. While we have been conditioned to think of it today as vaguely uplifting political poetry, our Founding Fathers began the U.S. Constitution with three purposeful words: "We the people."

The people are supposed to be in charge, with everyone operating under clearly stated laws equally applied. Similarly, the responsibility for the future of the Republic doesn't rest with presidents or mayors, governors or senators, but with each of us as citizens.

And yet ... we have been distracted. For too long, too many of us have been lulled to sleep or merely pointed in the wrong direction. The citizens have been told to fight with each other over the table scraps offered by the self-established ruling elite.

For more than 20 years in Texas, there has been Republican domination of the state's political machinery. For two decades, Republicans have held every statewide executive office, every statewide judicial office, and commanding majorities of both the House and Senate. Yet government is more bloated than ever, and the tax burden higher than when they took control.

When citizens raise these points, the elected class in Austin raise often their eyebrows in horror and tell of the dastardly deeds of the Democrats. Some, if they are edgy, might even lay blame on the "RINOs"—Republicans In Name Only. But here's the thing: everyone in office is a Republican in name only.

The fact is, conservative policies are killed or ignored in Texas because Republicans allow it. When a Democrat is seen gleefully holding a bloody knife over a gutted GOP priority, it is because Republican lawmakers handed them that knife.

Citizens must understand the process and not be distracted by the self-serving fairy tales told by lazy legislators.

It begins by reminding ourselves that the responsibility for safeguarding our Republic and advancing our priorities rests with each of us as citizens. We must not allow ourselves to be distracted by the public servants from our high calling as citizens.

JUST A SMALL BIT OF LIBERTY?
Even the sincere tyrants, the benevolent tyrants, are still tyrants.

You might remember "15 days to slow the spread," which became months (years!) of government restrictions and mandates. Millions were unemployed and untold thousands of small businesses vanished.

We were told to give up some of our freedoms and accept the imposition to serve a manufactured notion of the greater good. Once the mandates and restrictions began to lift, we saw that whatever their intentions, the result was an erosion of liberty and extension of suffering.

The experience stands as a sad indictment of how little our fellow countrymen value our Republic's hard-won liberties. We allowed governors to become feudal lords, mandating restrictions that would have once been unthinkable, or at least required legislative debate. In terms of practical governance, the chest-thumping conservative bastion of Texas was revealed to have much more in common with the leftwing realm of California than the Lone Star State's public relations would suggest.

Too many of our countrymen—even conservatives—succumbed to the idea that it is possible to sacrifice a small bit of liberty to the false god of safety and the public good.

Such a notion didn't arrive overnight but has been woven slowly into the fabric of our culture. We have rejected

God, and therefore the notion of inalienable individual rights.

History is abundantly clear: When individual liberty—even a small bit—is made subservient to the politically contrived "public good," only pain and suffering will be the result.

Whether it was Democrat icon Franklin D. Roosevelt sending American citizens of Japanese ancestry to internment camps and seizing their property, or Republican Texas Governor Greg Abbott unconstitutionally seizing the power to close small businesses, the claimed "good" cannot be found with the most powerful microscope.

Sacrificing individual liberty for the sake of what a politician decrees as the "common good" is to say that liberties originate from government and not God. And what government gives, government can take away.

As C.S. Lewis once noted, when "moral busybodies" determine what is good for everyone, everyone ends up suffering. When a benevolent tyrant torments us for our own good, he is still tormenting us.

An honest review of the lessons from the COVID years should lead us to firmly reject the tyranny of the politically defined public good. But will we?

Tyrants find it easy to nibble away at small bits of your liberty until all that remains is your subservience. The whole of history shows, in contrast, that the "common good" is best served by enhancing individual liberty.

As a self-governing people, we must stop acquiescing to the politicians and moral busybodies. We must daily assert our commitment to preserving the inalienable liberties granted to us by God.

KINGS DIE
Good intentions are no match for God's provisions.

Governments are instituted among men, the Declaration of Independence correctly notes, in order to secure our inalienable rights. Too often, of course, we have ended up creating (or tolerating) governments destructive to those purposes.

It should not surprise us God had strong recommendations for His people about how to correctly institute civil government.

For starters, He gave them what we would recognize as a highly decentralized system—no king or other supreme leader. The people were to be self-governing under the framework of laws He provided them as their eternal King. Disputes were to be handled communally, by judges who everyone recognized as wise and impartial.

To say this made Israel unique would be a vast understatement. Every other nation-state was led by a king —often one with delusions of divinity and a decidedly dictatorial bent.

Israel was a self-governing people for 400 years before they looked around and saw they were different. So they demanded that their most popular judge and prophet appoint for them a king; they rejected God.

Yes, they knew a king would tax them, send their sons into unnecessary wars and their daughters into servitude. Even knowing that, they wanted a king anyway.

And so they ended up with Saul, perhaps the most tragically self-destructive man in the Old Testament. He was sure he was God's gift to Israel, and he delivered as king exactly as advertised: taxes, wars, and a shift of culture. Whatever good intentions Saul might have had were overwhelmed by the corrupting nature of power. It's not so much that he was a bad king (though he became one), it is that as a king he was competing against God.

In the end, Saul wasn't killed in a palace coup; he was the victim of his own wars. He either committed suicide to avoid capture by his enemies (1 Samuel 31), or he was slain by an opportunistic foreigner (2 Samuel 1). However he met his fate, those enemies hung the bodies of Saul and his sons from the walls of Beit She'an in shame.

Saul no doubt envisioned himself a wise and benevolent man who possessed the wisdom to lead Israel despite God's warnings. Saul certainly never imagined his own corpse ignobly strung up like the hide of an animal. The walls of Beit She'an still stand, while Saul's memory lasts only as a cautionary tale.

We reject the gift of self-governance at our own peril, and frankly to the peril of those we would puff up as monarchs. Good intentions—theirs or ours—are no match for God's perfect provisions. There can be no "good government" apart from self-governance.

PEOPLE-PLEASERS
We live under the government we tolerate.

Our Founding Fathers upturned the traditional role of "the people" in relationship to "the government." The citizenry became the masters and government officials were to be their servants.

All good servants share a particular trait: They want to please people. That is not a bad thing, in and of itself. It is actually a very good thing.

Our system of government was designed to attract people-pleasers. In their obsession with checks and balances on power, the framers of the Republic wanted public officials to be those who yearn for the approval of their civic masters.

Yet a curious thing has occurred: Our Republic has devolved. The process by which we select public servants remains the same, putting people-pleasers into office. And yet, the structures of government and the miseducation of the people, mean once the politicians are in office they start trying to please those who show up—the cronies, the lobbyists, and the other politicians.

Whatever lip service they pay to "working for you," they functionally see themselves as servants to the head of their legislative chamber, their mayor, governor, or party leader. They get their information from lobbyists and hope to receive applause from the establishment-run media.

This is not how the system is supposed to work, but it is the system we tolerate.

The politicians are the same people-pleasers we elected ... they are just seeking approval from the wrong people. And one way they please those people is by stomping on the rights of the citizens. The servants have turned themselves into the masters—and we've allowed it.

As a self-governing people, we must recognize the role we have played in this reversal. We pay just enough attention to elect to office the guy or gal who has the most soothing voice, or tickles our ears with the right poll-tested catch-phrases ... and then we check out.

We allow the politicians to escape to the "backrooms" where they meet with "stakeholders," only to emerge with a "done deal" to which they had foolishly "given their word." And we then join in applauding their violations of our Republic's most cherished principles as evidence of "leadership" and "statesmanship."

It is time for the citizens to stand up and speak out. We must remind ourselves, each other, and most especially the politicians, that their job is to serve the people—and not the other way around. The citizens must exert themselves like never before, raising our voices and encouraging others to do likewise.

It is time for the politicians to remember they exist to serve. You and I need to be about the business of reminding them.

HYPOCRITES' CHAIR

It's time to stop coddling politicians, and start calling them out.

If anyone knows the name "Chorazin" today, it is only because it is twice mentioned in the New Testament for Jesus' famous "Woe to you" lines about the city. *Not exactly how you want to be known.*

It came to pass; Chorazin fell off the map for almost 2,000 years. Some people even doubted it ever existed. When archeologists in the early days of the 20th century discovered the village, they found not only the remains of a synagogue but an intact "Seat of Moses."

This was a common feature in ancient synagogues; it is where an esteemed teacher would sit, read from Scripture, and lecture. A replica rests in Chorazin's ruins today; I'm easily the least distinguished person to have sat on it. (The original is preserved in Israel's national museum; they won't let anyone sit on that one.)

In Matthew 23, Jesus mentioned how the "scribes and the Pharisees sit on Moses' seat," but he cautioned the people to "observe whatever they tell you, but not the works they do. For they preach, but do not practice."

Public hypocrisy, we find, isn't the exclusive domain of modern politicians.

But let's back up. For 2,000 years, the world has grown to see the Pharisees as the bad guys, as self-serving hypocrites. But that's not how they were viewed in Jesus' day; they were regarded as the right-thinking heroes of Israel—because they once had been. Through self-dealing corruption, they had begun to rot from the inside. Jesus was willing to call them out for what they had become.

It is also important to realize the Pharisees were as much a political institution as they were a religious one.

If anything, the Pharisees of Israel in the years surrounding Jesus' life were as well regarded by Jews as the Republicans in Texas have been for the last two decades. But like the dwindling devotion of some GOP politicians to their party's stated values and the grassroots base, the Pharisees had begun serving themselves rather than God and their fellow citizens.

You will recall Jesus described how the Pharisees did "all their deeds to be seen by others." Meanwhile, they "tie up heavy burdens, hard to bear, and lay them on people's shoulders, but they themselves are not willing to move them with their finger."

Can you relate? Today's politicians—Republicans and Democrats alike—want to be credited with the "righteousness" of so freely spending other people's money on their "good" causes. (Our national, state, and local debt is built on the photo ops of politicians and their cronies.)

Jesus' solution wasn't to coddle the governing hypocrites, but to expose them. He didn't tip-toe around their sensitivities, but called them a "brood of vipers."

When we as citizens fail to hold public officials accountable, we fail in our responsibilities. When we allow a continuing divergence between what politicians promise and what they deliver, we enable hypocrisy.

It is time for us to demand better, which starts by calling out the offenders, the hypocrites, and the cronies.

RULE OF LAW

Powerful institutions, even courts, will eventually serve only themselves.

History is replete with examples of judicial abuse and executive power exercised unjustly. Even in our own Republic, where we say the "law is king," we find horrible miscarriages of justice.

Yet none in history was more consequential than the trial and execution of Jesus of Nazareth during Passover the day before the Sabbath in the 1st century. Led before the Sanhedrin, the ruling council of Jews, Jesus' so-called trial was an exercise in railroading. The "court" had already decided He was guilty of being a troublemaker—He had healed too many people and even raised some from the dead.

Those things didn't do Him in, though. For the ruling elite, it was His incessant clamoring against religious and political corruption. That He claimed to be God was just icing on the cake.

The high priest, Caiaphas, told his colleagues before the trial, "It is expedient for us that one man should die."

Let's back up. Looking back 2,000 years, most people today think the Sanhedrin—presided over as it was by someone titled "high priest"—was a religious body. It was, but not only that. The Sanhedrin was a governing, political council, with enormous power over the daily affairs of life.

It was comprised of elders from the Pharisee and Sadducee political parties, serving functionally as an heir to the priestly judges in the Old Testament.

At its core, the Sanhedrin was a political body filled with politicians. As such, they were mostly concerned with protecting the status quo—that is, their own wealth and power. And for whatever else He was, Jesus was very much a threat to the status quo.

His trial violated a vast number of protections guaranteed under Israel's laws at the time. It started with a bribe, was conducted at night in the high priest's home, involved no valid indictment, excluded members of the Sanhedrin who might have voted no; the list goes on and on.

They wanted Jesus dead, and they broke their own rules to demand the Roman government carry out the execution.

While they were but players in the grand plan of salvation, the Sanhedrin's actions nonetheless serve as an important reminder that a self-governing people must be vigilant against the creeping cancer of corruption. Left to their own devices, powerful institutions will eventually serve only themselves—including the courts.

Institutions of government will serve the citizenry only for as long as the citizens themselves provide jealous oversight.

THE WRONG RESPONSE

Citizens have no obligation to praise politicians when they fail to perform.

Incumbent Republicans seem perpetually put out with the grassroots. The politicians are mad conservatives aren't appropriately appreciative for what we have been "given" by the ruling elite.

It is not uncommon to hear politicians and their sycophants suggest conservatives should just be "grateful for something rather than nothing." Party loyalists have enslaved themselves to the tyranny of low expectations, held captive to the politics of personality.

Rather than deliver fully and completely on their promises, too many politicians expect voters to rally around vague notions of party "unity."

We should all be for unity, but around *real* things. The best kind of unity arises when elected officials deliver without excuse on the promises they have repeatedly made. No one has an obligation—moral or otherwise—to unify around stale table scraps.

The implication by some in the crony wing of the Republican establishment is that voters should be grateful long-promised policies are being killed by "friendly" Republicans rather than those *mean* Democrats.

If one lives under a medieval monarchy or dictatorial oligarchy, then perhaps gratitude for benevolent neglect from the current regime is an appropriate response for the serfs. It could, indeed, be worse for them.

Fortunately, we live in a constitutional Republic in which the self-governing people are sovereign. Rather than preen around as "leaders," elected officials and government bureaucrats are supposed to be our servants.

Supposed to be.

The obligation is for them to deliver on our expectations and their promises. It is not the citizens' obligation to seek reasons to heap praise on politicians after they fail to perform.

Rather than pretend table scraps are a delectable meal, political activists must have high standards for—and expect real results from—our elected servants. Otherwise, no one should be surprised when voters start looking for new servants.

The wrong response is to replace bad Republicans with worse Democrats; but that isn't the only choice.

Consider this: In Texas, 85 percent of voters do not participate in party primaries. They have no loyalty to a political party. So it is safe to assume they don't care much about the unity of a political party, either. They are, however, very concerned with actual, practical results they can see for themselves and their families.

Our reaction to the faithlessness of politicians should not be to let our frustrations pull us deeper into the soft tyranny of the left. Instead, we should use those frustrations to set higher expectations for our public servants... and find better replacements.

The answer isn't to replace Republicans with Democrats. Instead, we should swap out self-serving politicians of all kinds for those who will fight unceasingly for the principles on which they campaigned.

TWO-CARD MONTE

Yes, there are two political parties—but they aren't what we are told.

Every day we are treated to relentless messaging around the fight between the Elephants and the Donkeys. We must be invested in that fight, we are told, and that fight alone. We have to choose one of those sides.

An old street hustle is three-card monte, in which the con artist distracts you with a game while robbing you blind. In politics, we're encouraged to watch the games between the Elephants and the Donkeys—even as our Republic is stolen from us.

Yes, there are two political parties, but they aren't what we are told.

The two real parties in politics are the ruling elite, and everyone else. Understanding that is critical to being an effective grassroots activist. The hustle, of course, is making us disbelieve the evidence of our eyes.

For example, it is why—after two decades of Texas Republicans promising to cut property taxes and reduce the size of government—property taxes are nonetheless 181 percent higher, and government has never been bigger. All while those same Republicans have held all the policy-making power in the state.

It is why Democrats, despite their messaging against accumulated wealth and the evils of corporate America, are nonetheless enriching themselves while enjoying the support of those same corporations.

Now, let's be clear: there are differences between the Republican Party and the Democrat Party. A casual look at their stated platforms and policy positions reveals starkly different approaches to government.

Yet those sales documents, those brand descriptors, rarely apply to the Republicans and Democrats holding offices of public trust. The politicians are more interested in building themselves up among their fellow politicians than delivering on the promises they made to fight for their constituents.

The public policy fights on issues citizens legitimately care about are used by the hustlers to distract us from their efforts to consolidate power. Cutting taxes, controlling spending, protecting the border, improving education ... all of those matter to citizens, yet rarely get done because they don't serve the interests of the cronies profiting off government.

We must recognize our culpability as citizens. We have outsourced the management of our Republic to ego-driven con men. We give our vote to the men and women whose words tickle our ears, not to people willing to fight aggressively against the entrenched establishment. We've let the cronies convince us public policy is best conducted with the voters sitting passively in the bleachers while the politicians participate in a choreographed fight using folding chairs and stage-blood.

The politicians who claim to be fighting for you, yet haven't delivered, are players in a political hustle designed to deprive you of your liberty. The political parties are useful tools, but they are too often co-opted by self-serving politicians against the citizenry.

It's time to take the fight to them. Citizens must stop outsourcing the governance of our Republic to people more interested in their standing among the cronies than in delivering meaningful results.

We must no longer be satisfied with scripted zingers aimed at the other party. As citizens, we must demand—and be satisfied only with—meaningful actions and real results.

This sad game of two-card monte played by three-bit politicians will only come to an end when the citizens have had enough. No more games. We have a Republic to save.

YOU JUST DON'T UNDERSTAND
It's the politicians who don't understand who is in charge.

Politicians are at their most condescending when informing constituents that they "just don't understand." The comment inevitably comes when the constituent has expressed frustration that long-promised action on publicly popular legislation has yet to materialize.

The real problem is not that the citizenry doesn't understand the legislative processes, it's that citizens have come to understand all too well the lack of results.

Whenever politicians feel a growing criticism from the public, far too many lash out in exasperation with one of several versions of that "you don't understand" temper tantrum. One of my least favorite is, "You didn't attend the meetings at the Capitol where we hatched this idea so you cannot criticize it."

Well, definitionally, the overwhelming majority of the citizenry were not in those meetings. That does not, however, negate anyone's right to speak out about the results of policies under which we must all live. The arrogance of suggesting otherwise arises from a fundamental misunderstanding of the roles of citizens and elected officials.

In our republican form of government, the citizens are allowed to miss every single millisecond of government hearings, and yet still reserve their sovereign rights to opine loudly and vigorously about the results.

To the politicians' chagrin, that is the way our system was designed. Without exception, citizens are the masters in our Republic; elected officials are the servants. The First Amendment was designed specifically for political speech critical of the ruling class.

The job of the citizen is to set the expectations. It is the job of the public servants to get the job done.

The details of the legislative process are interesting and sometimes informative, but in the end those details—and even the process itself—can serve as a distraction by crony politicians more interested in serving themselves than serving the citizenry.

When the servants start making excuses or imposing demands on the people in charge, it's time to replace the servants.

It is up to the politicians to make sure their processes produce the results voters want. It is the politicians who refuse to understand a basic truth: the citizens don't want excuses, they expect and deserve results.

WHAT DO YOU EXPECT?

Stop settling for the low-bar results tepidly offered by our civic clerks.

Citizens seeking to impact public policy often do so shackled by the low expectations set by political cronies. It's time for the grassroots to raise our expectations.

We have been conditioned as citizens to treat politicians as our nation's leaders. They are not; they are the people's servants. Politicians are to "leadership" in our nation what the pimple-faced order-taker at a fast-food chain is to healthy nutrition. Only less so, because at least sometimes that order-taker actually does the work of bringing you a diet soft drink while you wait for your greasy burger and fries.

Of course, the politicians spend a lot of time and energy trying to convince you otherwise. They want you to think that by setting the policy agenda for you, they are doing you a favor. They have special insider knowledge about what is and is not feasible. Again, not dissimilar to that fast-food clerk who knows what things the cooks in the back really don't want to mess with making that day.

In the case of the fast-food joint, customers settle for what is available, or leave if they cannot get what they want.

As the citizen-leaders of our Republic, conservatives have been doing way too much "settling" for the low-bar results tepidly offered by our civic clerks.

Frankly, though, that is because we often treat government the way we treat lunchtime hunger as we drive past a fast-food joint. We enter with a vague notion that we're hungry, while knowing nothing on the menu is actually that good for us, and then let the clerk direct us to paying for what they want us to have.

As we approach government, we must do so with steadier resolve. As citizens, we cannot let our Republic's fate be limited by what the politicians say they will—in their time—get around to doing. We must set higher standards for them, and demand loudly that they be achieved.

You need to know what you expect. Rally your friends and family to your cause, and then communicate those expectations loudly, clearly, and without wavering.

Effective citizenship starts with knowing what you expect and not being satisfied until your priorities are accomplished.

AT THE CROSSROADS
Are we taking advantage of our location and vocation?

The city of Megiddo was of critical trade and strategic importance for seven millennia. Never heard of it? Yes, you have. We know of Megiddo by its Greek name, through the writings of John in the New Testament Book of Revelation: Armageddon.

No matter what one thinks of eschatology and biblical prophecy, Tel Megiddo tells us a lot about the opportunities we have if we seize them.

The city was occupied for some 7,000 years. As an archeological site, it is without equal. Layer upon layer of archeological record testifies to people taking advantage of their geography to influence the world.

Megiddo was in a valley that made for easy travel. One could literally touch the corners of the known world merely by living in Megiddo. All of the important trade routes came through Megiddo, and those who lived there drew immense power from controlling the intersection.

We all have such opportunities.

Each of us is placed somewhere in which we interact, directly or indirectly, with thousands of people. Where are you? Are you using your position—maybe your actual geographic position, or maybe a profession, skills, wealth, interests, or relationships—to influence the world around you?

Politically, grassroots conservatives in Texas have been frustrated with the do-the-minimum attitude of Republican lawmakers. As the world's tenth largest economy and the Union's second largest state, Texas is at the center of attention... yet state lawmakers regularly pass on the opportunities to show bold leadership in the eyes of a watching world.

As happens, Megiddo's importance eventually waned. The geopolitical reality of the Iron Age and the rise of the Roman Empire, all washed by and Megiddo fell away into rubble. It was uninhabited by around 500 B.C. Yet its name and legacy lived on as a literary tool and a rhetorical device. (Megiddo's place in future history, of course, is a different discussion.)

I choose not to believe the decline of our Republic is inevitable. I believe rejuvenation is possible. I know it is needed.

You and I must decide what we will do to make where we are count and be a force for good influencing the world. Will we resign ourselves to the "inevitability" of a leftist tyranny? Will we shrug our shoulders and head down the well-trodden road to serfdom?

Or, will the patriots rise up? Will we rededicate ourselves to those founding ideals of life, liberty, and the pursuit of happiness? Will we fight for what these United States can be? Will we fight for that more perfect union of self-governing sovereigns?

Will we, in the words of the Old Testament exhortation, be "strong and courageous" where we are?

Should the Lord tarry for 7,000 years, will we be remembered for squandering our place in history or for seizing opportunities? What you and I **do** next will be the answer to that question.

ACKNOWLEDGEMENTS

This collection would not have been put together without the insistence of *Texas Scorecard*'s CEO, Nathan Ofe, or the editing of Gabbie Shafer and Rae Liput. They are responsible for any errors or mistakes.
Just kidding.
Any errors you find are because I ignored their best attempts at correction. Special thanks to Brandon Waltens, who regularly provides excellent counsel when I ask, "Should I write this?"

I would be remiss not to express my deepest appreciation for Kaitlin Coxon and Amber Corley of Pale Horse Strategies for their work in designing the cover and developing a release strategy.

Back in the day, my amazing bride knew she was dating a writer, and then figured out she had married a zealot. She spends a fair amount of energy helping direct that zeal in the right direction—for which I remain grateful beyond words.

She and our three kids have patiently suffered through the death threats I received. They were stalked by creepy operatives working for bad people trying to unnerve me. They were inconvenienced by the death of a couple of family cars as I criss-crossed the state. And they were awakened by late-night calls from irate politicians.

Their good humor and cheer sustain me. They give me new reasons every day to fight even harder.

ABOUT THE AUTHOR

A former newspaper reporter, Michael Quinn Sullivan was a campaign operative, congressional staffer, and media trainer before becoming a think tank vice president.

He founded the largest grassroots activist organization in the Lone Star State before returning to his roots and publishing the *Texas Scorecard*, a news organization focused on state and local government.

The *Fort Worth Star-Telegram* once wrote Sullivan "slays taxpayer dragons in Austin ... When the heat is on in Austin, Michael Quinn Sullivan knows how to make it even hotter." *Texas Monthly* dubbed him "the enforcer" on their list of the 25 most influential Texans, while the *Dallas Morning News* called him Texas' most influential unelected Republican.

He is the author of the state's most-read daily email, the Texas Minute, and hosts a morning podcast of the same name.

Michael and his wife have three adult children, a son-in-law, and a dog.

Made in the USA
Middletown, DE
08 October 2024

62236532R00080